Also by Michael Munn:

Kirk Douglas

Charlton Heston

The Hollywood Murder Casebook

The Kid From the Bronx:
A Biography of Tony Curtis

The Great Film Epics

All Our Loving (with Carolyn Lee Mitchell)

Trevor Howard
The Man and His Films

Michael Munn

Scarborough House/*Publishers*

In memory of Patrick Newell
1932-1988

Scarborough House/*Publishers*
Chelsea, MI 48118

FIRST AMERICAN EDITION 1990

Copyright © 1989 Michael Munn
All rights reserved
Printed in the United States of America

Library of Congress Cataloging-in-Publication Data

Munn, Michael.
  Trevor Howard, the man and his films /
Michael Munn. - 1st American ed.
      p.   cm.
  Includes bibliographical references and index.
  ISBN 0-8128-4006-2
  1. Howard, Trevor, 1916-1988. 2. Actors -
Great Britain - Biography.
  I. Title.
PN2598.H74M86   1990
792'.028'092 - dc20   90-41123
  [B]   CIP

Contents

Appreciation

WITHOUT THE ASSISTANCE of a good many people, I would never have been able to complete this biography. Not all the help I sought was forthcoming, so I am entirely indebted to those who were gracious and enthusiastic in their willingness to recount their personal experiences and impressions of Trevor Howard. These are in addition to accounts given in recent years by others who have allowed me to interview them at length, some of whom have sadly passed away and who are as missed in today's world of entertainment as Trevor is. So my sincere thanks to Sir John Gielgud who wrote generously to me; to Harry Andrews who didn't hesitate to talk at length; to John Leyton and James Brolin for their candid memories; to Dame Anna Neagle, William Holden, Barbara Kellerman, Roger Moore, Jack Cardiff, Kenneth More, Greg Smith, Val Guest, Robin Nedwell, Diane Keen and José Ferrer who have all spoken to me of Trevor over the years; to Marguerita Annis for graciously acting as go-between with Miss Helen Cherry; to my friend and colleague Ken Ferguson, Editor of *Photoplay* magazine, for his own personal recollections and for allowing me access to *Photoplay* material; to Michael Coupland and Trevor Harvey for their knowledge and experience, and to James Sharkey for providing me with a list of Trevor's film, TV and theatrical credits. And, of course, to Trevor Howard, not least for a memorable drink and a chat.

But most especially of all to Patrick Newell who was the first to come to my aid when I began writing this book, and who died before I had finished. This book is dedicated to his memory.

Introduction

A SMALL, SLEEPY English village, not far from Elstree Studios, had come alive with the invasion by a film unit making a picture called *The Shillingbury Blowers*.

The village hall had been commandeered by producer Greg Smith and director Val Guest who surrounded it with trucks and generators. From these, giant cables snaked across freshly mown lawns to power cameras and lights inside the usually placid hall. The scene of many Women's Institute meetings and jumble sales was now transformed into a veritable mini film studio.

Beside the hall a small caravan was parked. It was nothing special. Just like any caravan generally seen careering down motorways en route to the seaside. Out of this caravan stepped a man in a cloth cap and baggy trousers held up by braces. He would not have looked out of place with a chip butty in one hand and a pint of beer in the other. My escort, the young unit publicist assigned to take care of journalists like myself on location for a day, saw the man in the cap and said, 'There he is now. Let me introduce you to Trevor Howard.'

Trevor Howard? The notorious hellraiser? What, this man who looked perfectly happy to wander alone with his hands in his pockets like someone roaming contentedly and aimlessly in his garden? The clothing which made him virtually unrecognisable was easily explained. It was simply his wardrobe for the role of Old Saltie in the film. But the caravan?

'It doesn't seem right that a big star like Trevor Howard should have to use such a tiny caravan for a dressing room,' said my escort. 'He must be used to big studio dressing rooms. But he never complains. All the other actors use the wash rooms in the hall but Greg thought Trevor ought to have something more private.'

As we approached him there was certainly no mistaking the famous ripened face beneath the unfamiliar cap. But, for a legendary hellraiser, he seemed remarkably quiet, and even his cordial greeting displayed nothing of the man famous for his 'roar'.

I was introduced as a journalist from *Photoplay*, come to do some interviews.

'Is he now?' said Trevor, most probably wary of another reporter he'd never met looking for an angle.

There followed a few moments of small talk – how nice the weather was, how well filming was going. Then, from inside the hall the voice of the assistant director bellowed 'Lunch!' Trevor sauntered off towards the pub which had become the established watering hole for most of the actors and crew who preferred not to take advantage of the mobile catering facilities offered.

I followed the tide of people making for the pub and found Trevor sitting in a quiet corner. There was not the expected gathering around him, listening to uproarious and outrageous tales from this obviously highly esteemed and respected personality. Just an occasional 'Hello, Trev' from a technician or two, as well as from his younger co-star Robin Nedwell. On all counts, *not* the 'hellraiser' I'd expected.

I offered to buy him a drink. He beamed, lifted his empty glass and said, 'Ah, very good, amigo. A Whiteshield Worthington please.'

What followed was more of an amiable chat rather than a formal interview, although he generously allowed me to ask questions which he duly responded to. Perhaps it was hardly in-depth stuff, but the atmosphere allowed him to relax and be as casually pleasant as he liked. In this way I believe I got to discover more about him than I could have done from any pre-arranged, formal, 'in-depth' interview.

I've no idea how he would have been in an interview recorded for posterity on a tape-recorder, because I never got to meet him again for that purpose. In fact, the hour I spent with him in 1979 over a couple of beers was the only time I ever met him. But I have noted that most personalities when interviewed accept the fact that it's all really a 'set-up', when a superficial, usually temporary, friendship has to be immediately formed and, more often than not, broken within the space of an hour or so. Talking to Trevor Howard, however, I felt he was, at that particular time, happy to accept my presence and my questions without the need to perform or pretend in any way.

Not that he really ever needed to perform for the sake of the Press. He seemed to have his own way of dealing with reporters, usually by telling them exactly what they wanted to hear, whether it was true or not. He often led them a merry dance, up and down the garden path, with all sorts of stories; not in the style of a raconteur, more like one who enjoys teasing gullible pressmen.

For instance, once when catching a plane bound for Hollywood, he told the gathered newsmen that he wasn't coming back. He knew that's what they wanted to hear and they wasted no time in reporting that Trevor Howard had deserted Britain. But then he had the last laugh: he finished his job in America and promptly returned to his home in the village of Arkley where he lived with his beloved wife, actress Helen Cherry.

It was said by one particular show business writer that if Trevor Howard ever kept a press cuttings book, it must be very dull: he never did anything remotely scandalous, had won no Oscars, no fan magazine awards – only consistently good notices.

Well, he did keep press cuttings but his life was certainly anything but dull. No scandals perhaps. But dull? Never.

Not that he could be expected to remember every event in a full and exciting – and, for him, I think, rewarding – life. Many of his memories tended to be rather blurred (actors, it seems, are expected to remember everything as well as their lines), and although he kept press cuttings, he never seemed to be able to find them when it mattered. When Terence Pettigrew interviewed him at his home in Arkley, not long after I met him, Trevor was forever disappearing to go in search of some press cutting or other to nudge his memory and help him answer Terence's questions. More often than not he couldn't find what he wanted. He told Terence, 'If Helen had been here today it would have been different. She knows where everything is. Without her, as you can see, I just muddle through.'

Had he ever attempted to write his autobiography, he would probably have had almost as difficult a job documenting his life as any biographer would. But Trevor never wrote his autobiography.

Probably because he was far too honest: if he didn't recall an event or some particular fact, he said so. He was also far too unassuming to dress up his life and he was never a true raconteur. But he did tell some lively stories, usually to the people he worked with. So I am indebted to those who passed some of the stories on to me.

I'd like to think also that a good deal of what I discovered about the man came from sitting with him in that village pub. And it wasn't necessarily from what he said.

I'm glad I had that opportunity back in 1979 because, now that he's dead, his words and what I simply observed of him are all I have to go on first hand.

I haven't previously published what he told me that day, so this book is the first opportunity to put into print some of what he said, and sketchy as his words were in our short meeting 10 years ago, they must tell as much of his own life story as is possible.

One of the things he did say (and which I believe he said often) was, 'I've often thought of acting as being a wonderful job that gives me an opportunity to drink with some really good friends in exotic places around the world.'

This, then, is about the man himself, and about his work in the theatre and cinema that gave him that opportunity to drink with friends in exotic places.

1

A Sneaky Actor

WE'D SAT CHATTING for a while, talking a bit about *The Shillingbury Blowers*, and I mentioned how much I admired his performance as Captain Bligh in *Mutiny On The Bounty*, which I think both pleased and amused him. That had to be one of the most difficult films he'd ever made.

It seemed like a good moment to ask him if he minded if I threw some questions at him.

'Not at all, old boy,' he beamed.

I began asking him about his work long before even daring to broach the subject of his hellraiser image or of his childhood.

'My childhood?' he explained when I did get round to it. 'That's going back a bit. What I remember most about it is I was always on the move. My father worked for Lloyd's of London. He had a regular job and a regular income, but he usually worked abroad. Never saw him from one year to the next and I never really knew him.'

He didn't show it, but there was obviously a tinge of regret about his relationship – or lack of it – with his father, Arthur Howard-Smith. Much of what Trevor said, except perhaps to those closest to him, was only about the good things in his life – the people he enjoyed working with, the happy times he had. Try to get a bad word out of him about anything or anyone, and nine times out of ten you'd fail. Much of his childhood was spent in abject loneliness, and it seemed he preferred not to dwell on it. And at that time I wasn't prepared to push him.

Of course his father was not calculatingly negligent. Materially, he was able to provide his wife Mabel and their two children, Trevor and Merla, with all they needed. Trevor was accustomed to money and never wanted for anything – at least, anything that money could buy.

Patrick Newell, the British character actor who knew Trevor well and worked with him on a number of occasions, told me:

> It's an old-fashioned thing to say, but Trevor started off well educated and used to money. When he started working as an actor he probably didn't have a lot of money then, but he had a background, and so when he did start earning money it wasn't something he wasn't used to. He just carried on as he always did, but earning more money. I don't think money ever really meant that much to Trevor.

Life, as they say, is all swings and roundabouts, pros and cons, taking the rough with the smooth. For Trevor, childhood may not have been a time of financial deprivation, but he was certainly deprived of a father's guiding, guarding hand.

It didn't help that his mother had a severe case of itchy feet: she constantly wanted to travel. Arthur's income was certainly sufficient to allow her such a luxury, and so as a very young child Trevor was treated to the sights and sounds of far-flung countries. But what he may have gained in being able to travel so much in infancy, he lost in terms of a home. He had no roots. It seems only by mere chance that he was born in England and not in Ceylon where his father was usually based. Cliftonville in Kent just happened to be where his parents were on 28 September 1916, when Trevor Wallace Howard-Smith was born.

It almost seems like a quirk of fate that Arthur Howard-Smith and the former Mabel Wallace met at all. She was born in Canada but left home during her teenage years to train as a nurse in America. When she qualified, she satisfied her wanderlust by becoming a private nurse, working for rich American folk who, more often than not, travelled the world. This life continued, it seems, until she met Arthur Howard-Smith who was working in Ceylon.

'I think my parents met on a ship,' said Trevor, then added vaguely, 'or somewhere or other. I don't really know.'

Wherever it was, they made it to England where they

married, and where Trevor Howard-Smith eventually came
into the world. Not that he could ever have had any infant
memories of England since he was shipped off to Ceylon with
mum and dad while still a baby. It was in Ceylon that
Trevor's sister Merla was born.

Trevor did not tell me much about his childhood, but he
told Patrick Newell something about it when they were
filming *The Long Duel* in 1965. That film (though shot in
Spain) was set in India and certain aspects of the film brought
back childhood memories:

> The thing I remember Trevor telling me was to do with
> elephants which we had a number of on *The Long Duel*.
> He really loved the creatures. Absolutely loved them. So
> I asked him one day why he liked them so much and he
> said that when he was a boy living in some big hotel in
> Ceylon, he was taken by his parents to a Buddhist temple
> during some religious festival. And there were all these
> elephants and they were considered sacred. They were
> given a red carpet to walk on and he just thought they
> were magnificent. I suppose that memory stayed with
> him. He really treats elephants with respect. I thought it
> was remarkable.

When Trevor was five his mother wanted to travel again for
the first time since he had been born. She packed her things
and, with her two children, boarded a ship bound for the
United States. Arthur remained in Ceylon to continue his
work.

For six months they lived in San Francisco and then they
moved on to Canada, visiting Mabel's family. A year later
they moved back across the border to live in New York for a
time, and that's where a new love came into Trevor's life.

'I've always loved jazz music, for as long as I can remember
anyway,' he told me. 'New York in that sense was an
education for me.'

It was about that time that Mabel decided Trevor needed a
more academic education, so she brought him to England and
placed him in the very capable hands of the junior school
tutors at Clifton College, Bristol. At the tender age of eight

he was left alone at Clifton College while Mabel returned to Ceylon with Merla. One can only wonder at the confusion and emotional turmoil of a small boy who'd not seen his father for three years and who was now left virtually alone in what was to all intents and purposes a strange country. As I sat with him, he was loath to talk too much about it, but he did say:

> When I was at school I was literally on my own. Merla and my mother used to return to England during the holidays and on occasions my father came too. But a lot of the time during summer holidays I stayed in seaside bed and breakfast lodgings run by landladies – like the ones you see on seaside postcards!
>
> I had one housemaster who decided one year I should go home with him to spend the holidays with his mother and sister. They lived in Cambridge and I loved it there with them. I'm sure when it was time to leave them, I didn't want to. But that was all a long time ago, old boy. What'll you drink?

He allowed himself a chuckle at the memory, belying any sadness at the thought of those early years.

Being so young and without a family environment was bound to have some effect. In Trevor's case it would seem to have helped him along the road to independence. It was probably a case of sink or swim, but despite this there must have been an enormous hole in his life. Not surprisingly, for many years he considered the college his home, and he always had a soft spot for the place. There could be no doubting the college's ability to supply him with the kind of education his parents were paying for. But there was a little of the rebel in him. Not that he was a troublemaker, but he did resist efforts by his tutors to get him to take an interest in his academic studies. As he saw it, lessons only got in the way of more important pursuits like cricket, which he was fanatical about, and boxing at which he excelled. He may have resented being at Clifton College, all alone with no family, for the primary purpose of being educated, but what the college did offer were excellent amenities for anyone with a sporting attitude. And Trevor certainly had that.

Now, it's usually about this point in an actor's biography that the inevitable participation in school plays creeps in, but not in Trevor's case.

'Never thought about being an actor, amigo,' he said. 'Not then anyway. Too busy with more important things like cricket to even think about being in a school production of any kind.'

But didn't he ever appear in at least one play at school?

'Not one. Only started thinking about being an actor when I began sneaking out of school after hours to go to the local theatre and rather audaciously decided that I could do as well if not better than the actors I saw.'

All that sneaking off only began to happen towards the end of his time at Clifton. Before that he was torn between trying to decide whether he should play cricket professionally or join the RAF when he left college.

He continued to prove a rather dismal scholar but many of the masters seemed willing to overlook his academic short-comings because, when it came to a cricket match between schools, Trevor was invaluable to their team.

Then, at the age of fifteen, Trevor was able to discover jazz all over again.

'The time I really got to know jazz was when I was invited by an aunt in America to come and spend the summer holidays with her,' he said. 'I went to New York and lied my way into clubs and speakeasies to watch people like Louis Armstrong and Duke Ellington.'

Back home at Clifton, the adolescent Trevor developed new interests. Patrick Newell told me, 'Trevor was always rather strait-laced about sex but he did meet a girl at the college – a maid or a nurse or something – and they began going together. He said they used to climb out of the dormitory window after curfew.'

It was also around that time he started going absent without leave to the local theatre. Whether or not he was actually sowing a few wild oats only he (and the girl) would ever know, but he was certainly beginning to sow a few seeds of theatrical ambition that would eventually grow strong enough to overwhelm even his desire to be a cricketer. And that was a complete shock for everyone who knew him.

However, when he did leave Clifton College, he still wasn't really sure exactly what he wanted to do for a living, and he made some half-hearted attempts at a number of job interviews. Then he decided he would become an actor.

He knew the best place to study acting was RADA. Just how he managed to break into such an exclusive acting school without ever having performed in a single play remains a mystery, but he was nevertheless enrolled. Somehow he managed to convince them he was actor material: they must have seen something in him that was to make him one of Britain's most compelling actors.

2

No Better Petruchio

'PEOPLE SOMETIMES FORGET, old boy, I'd been acting for about 10 years before I did *Brief Encounter*,' Trevor said. 'My first job was doing a walk-on bit in *Revolt In A Reformatory* with Alastair Sim who I got to work with again in a film called *Green For Danger*.'

That professional début was in the summer of 1934, during his second year at RADA. The play ran for a month at the Gate Theatre and if anyone in the audience was interested enough to know who the young man with the red hair and no dialogue was, they'd find him in the programme as the one who played '2nd Boy'.

Other parts followed in the same year, and with each play his roles grew larger in both RADA and professional productions. He did *The Drums Begin* at the Embassy Theatre, followed by *Androcles And The Lion* at the Winter Garden Theatre and, for RADA, *The Faithful* and *Alien Corn*, both at the Westminster Theatre.

During 1934 his mother returned to England with Merla for good, although Arthur was still having to work abroad, writing to Trevor every week. But even this regular correspondence and the occasional visit by a father who was all but a stranger to Trevor did little to develop any kind of real father-and-son relationship. Trevor just didn't know his father. In fact, the closest he every grew to any of his family was perhaps to his sister, Merla. Trevor told me, 'I did have some strong family ties. Merla and I were very close and she was an actress for a while until the War came along. Then she gave it up. We were always close really.'

He left RADA in 1935 and almost immediately came very close to landing a Hollywood film contract. While he was appearing in *Aren't We All?* at the Royal Court Theatre, he was spotted by a Paramount talent scout.

'Yes, it's true I was offered a five-year contract by Paramount,' he said. 'But I was rather a snob about it all, as we all were at RADA. We didn't think serious actors did films, and I wanted to be a serious actor. Making films was the last thing on my mind.'

So Trevor turned down a golden opportunity to break into films 10 years before he finally did. I asked him if he ever regretted it.

'Regret it? What's to regret? I've had a good run in films and I've even made one or two bloody good films.'

It's difficult to speculate what might have become of him if he had gone to Hollywood, but it's most likely Paramount would have tried to groom him to become another Ronald Colman or George Sanders – a matinee idol. And he may well have made a good career by doing just that. But he would never have had the opportunity to make any kind of a name for himself on the stage which he dearly wanted to do, and the British Film industry would have been deprived of one of its own legends.

By the end of 1935, with a number of successful credits to his name, including *Justice*, *Lady Patricia* and *A Family Man*, the Stratford Memorial Theatre were impressed enough to invite him to join them for their 1936 Shakespeare season, to play some small parts and also to understudy. He found it invaluable experience.

'I've never been a classical actor but I have done Shakespeare, as any actor worth his salt should,' he said. 'I think it's true that Shakespeare is the best training an actor could have. I found that even just understudying, or when I did *The Taming Of The Shrew* (in 1947), taught me as much about acting as anything ever could.'

I'm sure that by 1979 it was a rare event to hear Trevor talk seriously about acting, especially to someone from the Press. While his attitude did change as the years wore on, in those early days prior to and for a while following *Brief Encounter* his work came before all else. He loved it and lived for it. But somewhere along the line he lost the motivation to become what could have been a great classical actor along the lines of John Gielgud or Ralph Richardson. As a talent he was arguably equal to our theatrical knights, but like James

Mason and perhaps Rex Harrison, it didn't help when he became caught up in a movie image that projected him more as a star than the accomplished actor he really was. Towards the end of 1936, when he finished his season with the Stratford Memorial Theatre Company, he landed a role in the incredibly successful West End run of *French Without Tears*. At first it had looked as though the play was doomed to failure. Written by the then virtually unknown Terence Rattigan and originally called *Gone Away*, the Criterion Theatre's director Bronson Albery put it on only in a moment of desperation to replace *The Lady Of La Paz*, an unexpected failure. It was John Gielgud who persuaded Albery to read Rattigan's light comedy about a French-language cramming school where a student's sister causes mayhem when she arrives and makes advances to all the young men.

Albery loved it and set up a deal with Rattigan's literary agent, A.D. Peters, to dip into his own pockets and invest in the production. Harold French was chosen to direct and he set about carefully selecting what he hoped would be a perfect cast. Trevor was enlisted to play one of the students along with Roland Culver, Robert, Flemyng, Percy Walsh, Alec Archdale and, as the girl, Kay Hammond.

There was still the lead role – the only student to see through the girl's mischievous plan – to be picked. Harold French chose Rex Harrison. The cast was complete, and, in the opinion of the director and producers, perfect.

For the first read through, the whole cast met in Albery's office with French and Rattigan, and it soon became apparent that Alec Archdale was a wrong choice so it was decided he be replaced by Guy Middleton. They also decided to change the title and came up with *French Without Tears*.

But the final dress rehearsal was a fiasco that very nearly turned the director into French Weeping Buckets of Tears. The previous rehearsal had gone fairly well, but on the night of the dress rehearsal, just 24 hours before it was due to play to a paying audience, the whole thing was an unmitigated disaster. Trevor, for one, dried up on only his second line. One actor completely forgot he was supposed to be a Frenchman, others fluffed lines and Rex Harrison seemed just about able to stagger through his performance.

Albery panicked, and had he been able to conjure up a miracle and replace the play with less than 24 hours to go, he would have, Harold French was furious and stormed backstage and ordered the cast to go through another rehearsal, and to get it right this time. And they did, to the great relief of both Albery and French. And of the cast.

The following evening they all gathered nervously at the theatre, dreading the fate that awaited if they performed less than perfectly. As it was, when the final curtain fell, the audience was cheering for more.

The play became a major success that ran for two years. For most actors a two-year run would be a godsend. But not for Trevor.

'That play was a marvellous break for me and Rex and we became good friends,' he told me, 'but doing the same play every night for two years was boring. I couldn't wait for it to end.'

Before the very final curtain fell there was an important event for Trevor: his father returned to England to retire. For the first time since he was five, Trevor had a complete family that seemed at last permanently settled. But he never was able to break down the barriers between himself and his father. He was now 21 and had made his own way in the world. He didn't need to go to his father for advice, and even if he'd needed to he wouldn't have. He loved his father, but he still didn't know him and he never was able to relate to, or confide in, someone who was a virtual stranger.

In 1939 he was again with the Stratford Memorial Theatre Company playing minor roles and understudying, and then, with the outbreak of World War Two, he decided to enlist.

'I always wanted to join the RAF, but for some reason they didn't want me,' he said, 'so I had a go at the Army, and they turned me down, too.' Eventually, though he did get called up. But before his call-up papers arrived, he set off for Colchester for three months, to help establish the Colchester Rep, and in the process star in *Private Lives* and play the Demon King in *Cinderella* – his first panto.

He returned to London to join the Harrogate White Rose Players, run by two ladies, Mrs Peacock and Miss Marie Blanche. He also found himself a girlfriend who must have been dismayed to find herself competing with his other loves – first acting, followed closely by cricket. On the other hand, she must have been enchanted by his impeccable manners and what were really rather strict moral standards. He was never one to allow a lady to pay the bill, walk behind him or stand while he sat, and as for sex, he positively disapproved of promiscuity, Even at RADA, where some of the girls were, by some accounts, as enthusiastic about hitting the sack as they were about treading the boards, he steered clear of women, believing he had to save every ounce of concentration – and probably energy – for his drama studies. However, when he finally met and fell in love with Helen they did in fact live together for a while before getting married. So Trevor wasn't against the idea of 'sex before marriage' – he just didn't believe in bed-hopping or chasing after women with anything like the enthusiasm he allocated for his other much-loved activities.

What is certain is that any young lady who attracted his attention enough to cause him to court her would have never found him anything less than gentlemanly, and his Harrogate girlfriend must have felt secure in the knowledge that the only rival she ever had to worry about was his work.

Trevor was also the kind of man who could enjoy a close relationship with a woman that didn't have to lead to anything more, and many of the actresses he enjoyed working with became good friends for life. One such actress was Dulcie Gray who, as a 21-year-old fledgling, joined the Harrogate White Rose Players and co-starred with Trevor in *The Importance Of Being Earnest*. It isn't too surprising that Dulcie, like a good many women who worked with him, should have responded to his charm and warmth, and it was only natural that at some time later Dulcie should expound on the gentlemanly delights of Trevor Howard to her friend, Helen Cherry.

The two elderly ladies who ran the Harrogate White Rose Players also thought the world of him, and they just couldn't bear the thought of losing him when his call-up papers arrived, even for the sake of King and Country. So Mrs Peacock and Miss Blanche made a point of forgetting to tell Trevor his papers had arrived. In fact, the papers met with a most unfortunate accident – in a fire.

Consequently the military police turned up and arrested Trevor. Since he had no intention of dodging the draft, in 1940 he found himself in the Royal Corps of Signals. He would have much preferred to be in the RAF. The Army tried hard to find him a job to which he was suited, and as he continually failed to grasp any of the basic skills each job required, he suggested they let the RAF have him. In turn they suggested he find a job he could do. When they tried him out with Coastal Artillery he spent three months proving they'd made a terrible mistake and finally convinced them that if they wouldn't give him to the RAF, they should transfer him instead to the Infantry. So off he went to the Officer Cadet Training Unit in Dunbar, Scotland.

'By a stroke of luck, the adjutant there was very keen on drama and thought he was a bit of an actor,' said Trevor. 'So when I turned up I suppose he thought this was his chance and he got me to put on a play which I directed as well as acted in with him in it, too.'

The play was *Rope* and it remained Trevor's only effort as a director.

This made army life much more bearable and he began to settle down and make friends. But it all fell into a pattern of monotonous routines and he began to wonder if he'd ever see any action.

Trevor was always quick to point out that there was nothing remarkable about his army days, and was forever embarrassed by a story put out by some insensitive publicist that he had been a Captain in the Airborne Division and had won the Military Cross. Trevor himself never subscribed to the myth that he was a war hero and hated the lie. He told me:

> It was just a load of crap for the sake of building up my image as some kind of hero. Obviously it was good copy for the papers, but there was never a grain of truth in it. I was bloody furious about it, and even now I still read about what a bloody noble hero I was supposed to be.
>
> The truth is I never saw any action. Would have loved to, not because I wanted to be a hero. I just wanted to do my bit like anyone else.
>
> I was actually in the Red Berets which had just been

formed. I'd heard they were looking for volunteers and I thought it would be more exciting than what I was doing, so I volunteered.

In 1942 he joined the Red Berets, officially called the Airborne Division, and he was given an emergency commission of Second Lieutenant, but, considering that the Allies wanted to end the War as quickly as possible, the military seemed in no hurry to send Second Lieutenant Trevor Wallace Howard-Smith off to war. Being a Red Beret seemed to consist of nothing much more than hurdling one assault course after another, and for a year following his commission he was continually tested and retested. The training had to be extensive and the tests he underwent with every other volunteer were severe and strict. Any sign of physical weakness meant the end of a Red Beret's chance of seeing action.

And that's precisely what happened to Trevor. After a full year's training some 'flaw' was detected, and on 2 October 1943 he was invalided out of the Army. He'd wasted three years. He was understandably furious, but what really shook and embarrassed him for the rest of his life was not so much the fact that he never actually fought in the War but that people should have been led to believe he was some incredible hero.

Even when he died, just about every obituary detailed the fictitious war record. This is especially surprising since out of all the profiles of Trevor Howard I have consulted, not one gives any mention of a Military Cross or any other similar detail. They all state clearly that he was invalided out of the war. While he would have preferred to have taken some active part in fighting for his country, he would have much preferred to keep the record straight.

Back in civvy street, he had to try and pick up the threads of a career that had been on ice for three years. In the process he met Helen. He explained to me how they met: 'I came across an old friend of mine who said "How would you like to play opposite a glorious redhead in the play, *The Recruiting Officer?*" and he got me a part. The redhead was Helen and we met for the first time at the cast gathering and I thought she was stunningly beautiful.'

Helen had heard all about Trevor from Dulcie Gray and she saw in him everything Dulcie had seen. Although he was attracted to her, he was reluctant to make any advances.

'I left it up to her to make the first move,' he said, 'When I fell in love with her, I felt like the luckiest chap in the world. Never been so happy, amigo.'

Not surprisingly *The Recruiting Officer* was one play Trevor always had a soft spot for, and when the chance came years later to do it on British television, he jumped at it.

So 1943 saw him in love and back to work. But this time all previous traces of his snobbery about acting in films had gone and he decided to try and break into movies.

'I'd heard they were making an important war picture, *The Way Ahead*,' he said, 'so I thought I'd write to the director Carol Reed along with my photograph, asking if I could have a part in it.'

He must have felt at the time that this was a worthwhile picture, made specifically for the war effort. The project was the idea of the Ministry of Information.

The Army had concluded that what Noel Coward had done for the Navy in his picture *In Which We Serve*, Colonel David Niven could do for them. Early in 1943 Niven was instructed to begin work with the Army's director of public relations to make a propaganda film that would make everyone sit up and take notice of the Army's effort to bring the War to a close. Negotiations began between Niven and the military PR on one side and Carol Reed on the other.

Reed had by this time become a highly respected director. When the War came along he joined the Army and, as a Captain, was assigned to the Army's Film unit, directing propaganda shorts. One of these films, *The New Lot*, written by Eric Ambler and Peter Ustinov, had taken a look at seven recruits who have to come to terms with Army life. In its way, the Army film unit was like a film studio and its own star system. Reed was a Captain, novelist Eric Ambler was a Major, and Peter Ustinov was a Private. Their contracts with the military were not unlike studio contracts: you didn't have the right to turn down work. Only in this case, refusal to work wouldn't mean suspension without pay, but time in the guardhouse.

As negotiations between Niven, the PR and Reed progressed, it was decided that they would expand on the theme of *The New Lot* by focusing on the lives of the seven recruits, plus one lieutenant to be played by David Niven, and produce it as a feature-length film called *The Way Ahead*. Deciding this should be a commercial venture as well as a piece of propaganda, they enlisted the assistance of a commercial company, Two Cities Films, to produce it while the Army supplied all the necessary military facilities.

The project smacked of class, and Trevor felt desperate to be a part of it. He wrote to Reed, and when it became obvious he wasn't going to get a reply, he drove to Denham Studios where filming was taking place and managed to gain access to the production office. He waited there until Reed finally showed up: it turned out that Reed had never seen Trevor's letter and, in the event, Reed didn't hesitate to give Trevor a role. He played a Naval officer whose ship is boarded by Niven and his men. It was a simple scene with a good quota of dialogue for Trevor. Brief though his performance was, it remains as vivid as anything else in the film, and memory seems to trick people into thinking he played a more prominent role. It has become quite natural, when recalling actors in the film, to roll off names like David Niven, Stanley Holloway, William Hartnell, Peter Ustinov, Trevor Howard, Leo Genn etc.

British audiences flocked to see it, but it didn't do at all well in America. The American distributors cut it from 116 minutes to 91, added their own introduction by American journalist Quentin Reynolds, and retitled it *The Immortal Battalion* when it was released in America in 1944.

For Trevor it was a real springboard into films, partly because of its stature, quickly earning a reputation as one of the best British war films ever made – some would say it was the best made anywhere. It also proved to him that acting in movies was just as respectable a vocation as working in the theatre. He discovered it required a whole new kind of discipline. There was a great deal of waiting around on the set while lighting, sound and camera were set up; and a day's filming captured little more than several minutes of film. But what he enjoyed was the fact that, unlike a long theatrical run, it didn't mean doing the same performance day in, day out for however many weeks. Each new day meant new dialogue, new scenes. All this suited Trevor very well and he was keen to make another picture. But until the film actually opened he couldn't expect producers to be knocking at his door.

It was also an important film for him because it established a firm friendship with Carol Reed, later to become Sir Carol Reed, and one of the most important directors of his era.

Before the film was premièred Trevor was appearing in *A Soldier For Christmas* at Wyndhams Theatre, followed by his performance as Mat Burlkey in *Anna Christie* at the Arts Theatre. During 1944 Helen was the seasonal leading lady with the Stratford Memorial Company, by which time she and Trevor were living together – a secret kept from the Press, the public and Helen's family. Trevor's somewhat Victorian standards may have dictated his generally non-promiscuous behaviour, but Helen was a woman he wanted to spend the rest of his life with and he intended to be with her every moment possible. He spent every available weekend with her in Stratford, living in a caravan she had rented. 'Living in sin' in those days really was a pretty shocking thing to do, and they both knew they couldn't keep it a secret for very long, especially from the family. So that year they married. Only the family and closest friends were there to witness the event on 8 September 1944.

Trevor never could get over his immense good fortune in finding a wife like Helen and in 1979 he said, as though he could still hardly believe it, 'We've been married for 35 years. What is that – a silver or platinum anniversary or something?'

His life with her was something he always preferred to keep out of the public eye as much as possible. They never became a typical show-biz couple and their private life was one seen only by friends and family.

Said Patrick Newell:

> They were very private people. He was married to her all along. There was never any sort of 'film star' thing with Trevor. He used to tear off for three or four days with a few of the lads and have a few pints, but he was never one of those woman-chasers. He and Helen were together for

ever. She was marvellous to him but then he was gentle and kind and reasonable.

They began their married life in a small flat in Pall Mall in London, close to 'theatreland', and both continued to pursue their careers, hoping in the near future to be able to buy their own house.

In 1945 Trevor was offered a small but telling part in *The Way To The Stars*, another wartime drama but this time focusing on the lives of men stationed at an RAF base. Its director was another of Britain's finest – Anthony Asquith – as prestigious a director as Carol Reed. Small though his role may have been in the film, this was another feather in Trevor's new film actor's hat.

It must have been an added thrill, having once dreamed of being a pilot, to step out onto the RAF station at Catterick, where many of the scenes were shot, dressed in RAF uniform. He found himself surrounded by talent: Asquith was behind the camera translating Terence Rattigan's screenplay onto celluloid, while in front stood such British luminaries as John Mills and Michael Redgrave.

Shooting his first scene with Trevor, John Mills couldn't help but be aware of this newcomer's presence and talent. When he arrived home that evening, he said to his wife Mary, 'I've just played a scene with a young actor who I think, with any luck at all, must become a star.'

Sir John Mills considers the film itself to be the finest Asquith ever made, and not only did it receive favourable reviews at the time but is still highly regarded by critics today. In 1972 Basil Wright wrote that it displays 'humour, humanity and not a sign of mawkishness'. Decidedly mawkish, however, was the title it was released under in America – *Johnny In The Clouds*. Its American distributors also added their own prologue to it, set after World War Two.

John Mills had said that Trevor just needed some luck. By now Trevor may well have felt that he'd used up his fair quota of luck for one life-time; he'd found Helen and was able to make a living at something he really enjoyed doing. But there was, it turned out, still some good fortune in reserve that was to set him off on a long and distinguished film career. It came in the form of *Brief Encounter*.

'It was just luck that Noel Coward chose me for *Brief Encounter*,' he said. 'It was luck I worked with Celia Johnson and David Lean. It was all just luck. What more luck could I ask for, old boy?'

Noel Coward set up the production himself as well as writing the screenplay from his one-act play *Still Life*. He had two co-producers, Anthony Havelock-Allen and Ronald Neame, and to direct it he chose the relatively new David Lean. Lean was still in his thirties and had only two screen credits to his name as director. Having graduated from tea boy to clapperboard boy to editor, he was Coward's choice of co-director for *In Which We Serve* in 1942. Still working with Coward, Lean directed solo for the first time on *This Happy Breed* and then *Blithe Spirit* before really making his mark with *Brief Encounter*.

It was Anthony Havelock-Allen who came up with the suggestion of Trevor Howard for the male lead in *Brief Encounter* after seeing him in *The Way To The Stars*. Both Lean and Neame agreed that Howard would be what they were looking for but it was Coward who had to make the final decision. The two co-producers and the director set up a screening of Trevor's scenes from *The Way To The Stars* for Coward to view. If Coward said 'no' there was no arguing the point. But after viewing the scenes Coward told them to go ahead and send Trevor Howard the script.

As for Celia Johnson, she was already cast as the female lead, having been Coward's personal choice. She had previously worked with him on *In Which We Serve* and *This Happy Breed*. Her fee for *Brief Encounter* was £1,000. Trevor received £500 – the difference between an established film star and a newcomer.

It was a simple story of a suburban housewife (Johnson) who meets and falls for a gentlemanly doctor (Howard). Their affair is short and poignant. Realising it can lead nowhere they decide never to see each other again. Although this was a story of adultery, Lean's handling of the love scenes was sensitive, making them genuinely touching and reducing 1945 audiences to tears.

Well, not all audiences. When it was previewed the audience kept laughing at the love scenes, and Lean was so anxious that he actually considered breaking into Denham Studios to steal the negative so that further prints could not be produced for general release. In retrospect, Lean believes the preview audience were laughing from some sort of nervous embarrassment at being treated to an adulterous love story. Whatever the reason, audiences who subsequently paid to see it loved it, and Lean can be justifiably proud of making what may arguably be considered his first masterpiece.

The film went on to win an award at the Cannes Film Festival and both Lean and Celia Johnson were nominated for Academy Awards. Surprisingly Trevor wasn't. But that may have had more to do with the fact that his role called for him to be little more than manly and considerate while Celia Johnson had opportunities to display much more anguish and emotion. What Trevor did with his role was probably too subtle to be considered outstanding. It's a style that established him as one of the finest of screen actors because he always made acting look so easy. Although he never did become what they call a 'box office attraction' he remained in demand for the rest of his life because, as any director, producer or actor will tell you, no matter how poor a film with him in might be, he could never give a bad performance.

Patrick Newell told me:

I've never seen him turn in a bad performance. I've seen him be really good in very bad films and I've seen him better than better in really good films.

It all stems from *Brief Encounter*. If you study that film it's all there. The warmth, the sincerity, the understanding he had of people. That's the secret of acting in a way. Some people have it more than others. A lot of actors go over your head and just think of themselves, and really they're pretty poor actors. A good actor can act with his back to the camera. It all works if you're sincere, even if your back is to the camera. It's how you say it that really counts and if you believe what you're saying. Trevor did.

It's all there in *Brief Encounter*. Everything. He's not

one dimensional. He's many dimensions. Just little bits he does. Even if one hand moved it meant something. He didn't plan that. It comes from believing it. Olivier plans every move, for instance. He never changes from one rehearsal to another. But Trevor was all from the inside. And then, of course, everything else worked.

Trevor, always so unassuming, said of the film's success, 'We realised at the time that it was a good film. It was honest, and it certainly had its heart in the right place. But great? That's not for us to say. If the public think it's great, then maybe it is. They are the ones who decide these things.'

Before filming on *Brief Encounter* had begun Rank, who were to release the film, had offered Trevor a contract that would have tied him exclusively to them. However, he asked for, and received, a non-exclusive contract allowing him to continue work in the theatre while making only one film a year for five years. By the time the film was finished Rank seemed to have lost interest in him, neither inviting him to the Press show nor sending him on the promotional tour with Celia Johnson.

He now came to the attention of Launder and Gilliat, a successful partnership between Frank Launder, a playwright who turned his talents to writing screenplays, and Sidney Gilliat who began his film career as an assistant director to Walter Mycroft and then as a screenwriter. Launder and Gilliat first joined forces as screenwriters and then, in 1945, as co-producers, calling their company Individual Pictures.

Individual's launch was with *I See A Dark Stranger*, and they considered Trevor Howard an ideal leading man to co-star with Deborah Kerr. Launder and Gilliat had agreed that they would take turns directing their films, and with this, their first, Launder kicked off in the directorial chair. It was a comedy thriller about an anti-English Irish lass, played by Deborah Kerr, who becomes an agent for the Germans during the War. But in the course of her mission she falls in love with an English officer, played by Trevor.

On location in Ireland Trevor was delighted to discover that the country was untouched by war rationing and there was no shortage of Irish whiskey. 'It wasn't at all bad,' he said with a note of understatement, 'so I smuggled some back to England!'

When released in 1946 the film proved popular and was well received by the Press, but American audiences, who saw it under the title *The Adventuress*, were baffled by some abruptness in exposition. Not for the first time – nor the last – had an American distributor taken a British film of the Forties, retitled it and cut it, in this case from 114 minutes to 98.

Launder and Gilliat had no second thoughts about inviting Trevor to join them for their next picture, *Green For Danger*, as a surgeon.

Alastair Sim starred as a detective investigating two clue-less murders in an emergency war-time hospital. There were six suspects and Trevor was one of them. This time it was Sidney Gilliat's turn to direct and under his guiding hand it became something of a classic comedy thriller with moments of real fright offset against the droll wit of Sim. It was the first film to be made at the reopened Pinewood Studios, closed during the War, and the studio bar became a regular oasis for social gathering. Trevor told me, 'I always like to end the day off in the bar with a drink with my friends. Sometimes from there we'd move off to a restaurant. I enjoyed it, and why not, amigo?'

Why not indeed, especially when drinking buddies would include some of the cream of British acting talent, such as John Mills who would have had the opportunity of toasting the success he had prophesied for Trevor and which seemed even more established when they came to make *So Well Remembered* at Denham in 1947. Set in a drab industrial town, the film was meant to be a drama of social significance, but it was all rather routine under the apparently nervous hand of American director Edward Dmytryck: Dmytryck must have been under some pressure at the time as he was about to be blacklisted in Hollywood as McCarthyism dawned.

Almost as soon as he had finished work on the Dmytryck film, Trevor went to work on *They Made Me A Fugitive*. This gave him his biggest starring role since *Brief Encounter*. In it he had a complete change of image, playing a demobbed pilot who is drawn into the black market and framed for a murder.

Escaping from Dartmoor Prison, he sets out to take vengeance on the gang leader who set him up.

It was a film that virtually launched a fashion for realism in British films. The roots of this realism were actually European: the film's director was Alberto Cavalcanti who had been an influential avant-garde set designer for a number of French films before coming to England in 1934 to make documentaries. He began directing feature films, introducing a documentary style to them, and it was this style that made *They Made Me A Fugitive* so innovative. (As a matter of interest, the American distributors felt their audiences would not be attracted to a film called *They Made Me A Fugitive* and retitled it *I Became A Criminal!*)

It was Trevor's first chance to break out of the 'perfect English gentleman' mould he'd been cast in, and in time he was to have opportunities to stretch himself in a variety of 'heavy' roles. Yet, with rare exceptions, whenever he played a heavy it was not without some of the characteristics that had endeared him to audiences. As Patrick Newell has noted, 'He had this warmth that even came across when he was supposed to be nasty. Who else could do that? He brought humanity to every part he played so the heavy roles were never really that nasty.'

It's always a cliché to talk about an 'actor's actor', but that is precisely what Trevor was. I have found it impossible to find one actor who didn't like working with him, or watching him perform. Even some of the big star names who would later make themselves unpopular with him could never deny that they thought him a marvellous actor. Even actors who have never worked with him and who may be totally out of his league can't help but admire him, so it should come as no surprise to discover that when Pat Wayne (son of Big John) was asked to name his favourite actor, he replied, 'Trevor Howard'.

Trevor was and is generally thought of as a film actor, but, once he was underway making films, he refrained from signing any contracts that would prevent him from doing stage work. However, he rarely returned to the theatre. In a short space of time his film star image inevitably overshadowed the amazing range that was usually only evident when he performed in a play. This makes it easy to forget that in 1947 he gave a performance that many would say was his finest ever: because it was never captured on celluloid and because his theatre work has been all but overlooked (you can hardly find a mention of him in reference books about the theatre), it has almost become lost to memory. Except by those who saw it and can never forget it.

It was as Petruchio in the 1947 Old Vic production *The Taming Of The Shrew* that he triumphed. *The Times* was moved to say, 'We can remember no better Petruchio.' And time and time again I have heard the same said by his peers. Harry Andrews told me:

Trevor was the definitive Petruchio. I was working with the Old Vic at the time Laurence Olivier invited him to come and do *The Taming Of The Shrew*. I was delighted because I knew Trevor from when he was in *French Without Tears* and I was in just a walk-on part. But we became friends then because we both had cricket in common. I didn't work with him again until 1947.

He was just magnificent as Petruchio, and so they offered him other great parts in the classics. But he was being offered film contracts which he accepted instead. I always thought that a great pity. He could have had a marvellous career in the theatre and that was a great disappointment to me. I would have loved to have seen him as Macbeth.

But he was a great actor, a great character and a friend. We used to meet and have a drink and I met Helen who was a wonderful wife and companion to him.

There is one story about him I always remember. We were in Birmingham in 1947 to open *The Taming Of The Shrew* at the New Theatre, and there I told him about an officer I knew in the army called Tiny Lewis. He was six foot five inches and a great boxer. I told Trevor that one of his tricks in the mess when he'd had a few was to stand upside down with a pint of beer and eat the glass.

This fascinated Trevor. He was riveted, and so when he came to Birmingham where Tiny Lewis lived he said, 'I have to meet him. Come on, ask this chap to come down and do this trick with a glass.'

I said, 'I don't think he does that sort of thing for
general entertainment, you know.'

But Trevor said, 'Go on, ask him.'

So I got in touch with Tiny and asked if he'd come
down and he said; 'Okay'. He came to see the matinee
and then he got everyone down below the stage and he
did his trick. Everyone applauded and Trevor loved it.
He never forgot that. Every time we got together he'd
say, 'Remember Tiny Lewis eating that beer glass?' and
he'd have a good laugh about it.

The whole company enjoyed tremendous success with *The
Taming Of The Shrew* which opened in Edinburgh, toured the
country and then went to Europe, closing in Brussels.

Trevor, as unassuming as ever; said about his remarkable
achievement, 'If anyone thought I was the best Petruchio,
that's very gratifying, but it's not for me to say, is it? I enjoyed
doing it but one feels one can always do better.'

As Harry Andrews said, after his stint with the Old Vic
Trevor went back to making films but it may well have been
an offer he couldn't refuse. For one thing, it was a picture for
David Lean, and it also meant a month or two filming in
Switzerland. And for Trevor some of the attraction of
movie-making was the opportunity it gave him to travel.

The film was *The Passionate Friends*. Although based on an
H.G. Wells book, it was no sci-fi spectacular but another tale
of romance and infidelity with Trevor playing something of a
variation on his *Brief Encounter* role. Ann Todd played a
married woman (to Claude Rains) who meets her former lover
(Trevor Howard) while in Switzerland and rekindles the
romance. Lean fashioned the film with his usual craftsmanship, making particularly effective use of flashbacks, and
extracting strong performances from his three key players.

During his free time Trevor took to the snowy slopes for
some downhill sports. He loved skiing, and he and Helen
enjoyed a number of skiing holidays in Switzerland in the
ensuing years. That year, 1948, was tinged with personal
tragedy, however. Trevor's father died in February. They had
never really grown close but it was nevertheless a loss for the
whole family.

3
A Wonderful Woman

'HAD A DRIVING offence or two, but I never broke the law by
smashing up pubs and restaurants,' Trevor told me when I
broached the subject of his so-called hellraiser image during
my interview with him. And then he added, 'But I did get
arrested while making *The Third Man* in Vienna.'
That beautifully ripened face of his cracked as he chuckled
at the memory. In Vienna he had been united with Carol
Reed for what has been described as possibly the greatest
British film made since World War Two – *The Third Man*.
Trevor recalled:

> One evening I discovered a place which had a band, and
> I heard music coming from it and just couldn't resist it.
> Problem was I was playing a British Military Police
> Chief, and I still had my uniform on when I turned up at
> this place. In no time at all I was conducting the band,
> having a few drinks and thoroughly enjoying myself.
>
> Some soldier saw me, realised I wasn't a real major
> and I suppose he thought I was impersonating an officer
> or whatever. Anyway, the silly bugger called the police
> and I was arrested.
>
> The next morning someone from the production office
> turned up and said, 'Please can we have our actor back,'
> and they let me go.
>
> It was a wonderful time. Wouldn't have missed it for
> the world. I loved making that film. It had so much talent
> – Carol Reed, Joseph Cotten, Orson Welles.

And let's not forget Trevor Howard. The image of Orson
Welles as Harry Lime seems to loom so large that most people
have an impression that he was on film. And while no one
could argue that his presence was totally captivating, Welles'

role was, in fact, relatively brief – it was Joseph Cotten who had the main role. He was the hack American writer who comes to Vienna looking for the murderer of his friend Harry Lime, only to discover Lime isn't dead but a black marketeer, and, in the final ingenious twist of the plot (of which there are many), kills Lime.

Trevor's role was that of Colonel Calloway who sets Cotten up as the bait with which to catch Lime. It was a role of many dimensions and one which probably stretched him further than any previous film. His colonel was a stalwart agent of justice, sarcastic and cynical and yet capable of compassion.

Also playing a major part was Italian actress Alida Valli, and a bit further down the cast list was Bernard Lee, most immediately remembered for his role as 'M' in the James Bond films. *The Third Man* was the first of a number of films Trevor and Bernie Lee worked on together, and from then on anyone who knew them realised that when those two got together there was going to be some high-spirited fun. Said Patrick Newell:

> Bernie Lee was a good friend of Trevor's. They used to do some outrageous things together when they'd had a couple of beers. Like they'd crawl across the floor in restaurants pretending to be a couple of dogs. Bernie would go 'Woof, woof!' and Trevor would bark back, 'Get off, amigo!' They didn't really care about what other people thought. But I never heard Trevor embarrass anyone, even if he'd had one or two.

Obviously the Vienna taverns became a regular haunt for Trevor who would usually be joined by Lee and sometimes Carol Reed. It was outside one of these taverns that Trevor heard an unusual musical sound that totally enchanted him. He went to investigate its source and discovered Anton Karas, a busker playing a zither. Trevor brought Karas and his zither to the attention of Carol Reed. It was agreed that the street busker's music would be perfect as the background score on the film's soundtrack. Thus an unknown street entertainer suddenly found himself in the role of film music composer, and his *Third Man* score, particularly the haunting Harry

Lime theme, remains instantly recognisable and has become completely identified with the image of post-war Vienna.

As for the film itself, that was born of a whim of British movie mogul Alexander Korda who wanted to make a film set in Vienna. Graham Greene wrote the story and screenplay and Korda made a deal with American David O. Selznick to co-produce it. Carol Reed, who apparently helped Greene to fashion his screenplay, was chosen to direct, and he turned in a film that owes much to the camera work of Robert Krasker with its inclined angles and constructive use of shadows and light. Add to all that Welles' own dialogue, and the strong performance of all the cast and you have a movie classic that is a truly collaborative effort.

However, typical of Hollywood's attitude to the work of British directors of that day, Selznick decided to refashion the finished film for consumption by American audiences. He cut the film from 104 minutes to 93, and replaced Reed's own introductory narration with one spoken by Joseph Cotten.

When the film was finished Trevor returned home to Helen. Any hopes that she might have him all to herself for a while were dashed: the lure of filming abroad was one Trevor found hard to resist, even if it meant being separated from his wife for a month or two. When Ronald Neame, now turning his hand to directing films, sent Trevor a script called *The Golden Salamander*, with locations in Tunisia, he once more packed his bags. It was a decision that led to the only real rift in their marriage.

The film was little more than a routine actioner with Trevor playing an archaeologist who goes off to North Africa, falls in love with a Tunisian girl and ends up a hero when he smashes a gun-smuggling racket.

In the world of film-making where men and women are brought together in close proximity, there often emerge relationships that lead to love affairs and even marriages. Movie history is peppered with examples like Bogart and Bacall, Burton and Taylor, Gilbert and Garbo, Tony Curtis and Christine Kaufmann, and countless others. Trevor had worked alongside some of the most desirable women in both cinema and theatre, and he formed friendships with many of them. Helen has been reported as saying that the kind of women he liked were the ones who could make him laugh. But very few of these friendships spilled over into his after-work hours. His way of life dictated that 'after-hours' friendships were usually with those male friends who liked to stay behind after a day's filming for a jar or two, and not even Helen seems to have infiltrated that part of his life.

But she always lived secure in the knowledge that however many drinks he might have over a period of however many hours (or sometimes days) she was the only woman he wanted to come home to. That is, until he went to Tunisia and word reached her that something was apparently going on between Trevor and his leading lady, Anouk Aimée.

Anouk was born in France to parents who were professional actors, so it wasn't surprising that she should follow in their footsteps. She was a graceful, feline beauty who had made a couple of French films before making her English-speaking début in *The Golden Salamander*. Anouk must have been someone who made Trevor laugh, because for once here was a woman whom he did tend to spend a lot more time with away from the set than usual. Not surprisingly the gossipmongers put the word about that the two were having an affair and this made superb copy for the Press. Such reports shocked and distressed Helen: for the first time she wondered if Trevor would come back to her.

Whenever Helen's own career allowed her, she went with him on location but, during the filming of *The Golden Salamander*, she had remained home because of work. Frustrated with worry she assumed the worst. It was a time of real unrest in their marriage. Over the phone Trevor assured her that the reports of an affair were untrue. It's certainly doubtful that he was involved with Anouk, although he did enjoy her company enormously. To anyone who has known Trevor it would seem inconceivable because, more than anything else, whether it was acting or cricket, he loved Helen. As he told me, 'Wonderful woman, my Helen. My life with her is the one I like to keep to myself. From the day she came into my life when we did *The Recruiting Officer*, there's never been a moment when I've not wanted her, and only her. Never fooled around, amigo. Never wanted to, never needed to.'

When he finished filming *The Golden Salamander* he was anxious to return home to patch things up with Helen. And from that time on there seems to have been no doubt in Helen's mind as to his loyalty. 'No matter what he was up to – and he travelled the world as a film star – I always knew he would come home to me,' she said some months after he died. 'I've never loved another man in my life and I think he felt the same about me.'

Although Helen never became the star Trevor did, she never begrudged him his success. She was always free to pursue her career and occasionally they did get to work together. But I think she saw her role as a wife being far more important than her career, and although she continued acting, and still does, she never let it intrude on their marriage. In a very real sense, she stood back to allow him space to enjoy, not just his career, but also his strictly men-only activities like cricket and drinking. But she was always there when he came home. The impression one gets is that, apart from his obviously exclusively male pursuits, he and Helen were two of a kind.

Harry Andrews said, 'Trevor was a very kind, very warm person. Always gentle with people. You often saw him in films bellowing at people, but he never did that in real life. And he always had time to speak to younger actors. He was always kind to them.' And Helen has always been just the same. Marguerita Annis, mother of Francesca, has been a long-time friend of Helen's, and she told me, 'Helen is just a very nice, very warm person. I first met her in the early Sixties when Francesca was making a *Flipper* film in the Bahamas, and Trevor and Helen were there, and Helen was enormously helpful to Francesca. Always courteous and willing to help. She was a wonderful person then, and still is now.'

It's not difficult to see why they were such a beloved couple – and absolutely perfect for each other.

4
Test Match, Amigo!

DURING THE FORTIES, Trevor had made his mark as an actor, both in films and on the stage. But the Fifties was the decade of Trevor Howard the film star, the personality, the character, even though few of his films during those 10 years were particularly good.

Perhaps it might have been a time for him to emerge as one of the giants of the British stage, but somehow he was swallowed up in the then flourishing British film industry, undoubtedly seduced more often than not by work in far-flung and exotic places. Or maybe it was just because somewhere along the way his ardour for acting began to fade. Said Helen recently, 'His real loves were myself and cricket. Acting came a poor third.'

Yet while many, like Harry Andrews, may lament the loss of a potentially illustrious name being added to the British theatrical heritage, I don't suppose Trevor himself ever did. True, he found himself starring in a number of mediocre films, but he managed to enjoy himself immensely at the same time. Perhaps part of it was because acting for him was never difficult – or at least, he always made it look so easy – and having established himself as a film star, he was happy to ride on the crest of that wave for as long as it lasted.

Making movies certainly proved a lucrative way of making a living and although there always seemed to be a paucity of really good scripts, there were plenty of bad to middling scripts being constantly offered to him. Of course, he always looked out for the better ones, or at least those that offered a chance to make a decent film, and when he read the screenplay of *Odette* that producer/director Herbert Wilcox offered to him he reckoned it was a film worth making.

In the true story of the incredibly heroic Frenchwoman, Odette, who worked for the French resistance during the

Nazis' occupation of France, Trevor's role was that of war-time hero, Peter Churchill. He accepted the part knowing that the film was really a star vehicle for Anna Neagle in the title role. The wife of her mentor, Wilcox, who had established her as a major star in a long succession of popular British films, Anna Neagle was at this time one of the biggest box office attractions the country had to offer.

Yet while Wilcox had obviously conceived the whole project with his wife in mind, she was actually more than reluctant to do it. When I had an opportunity to interview Dame Anna not long before she died, she told me that she had felt the responsibility too great at first to portray a woman of such remarkable courage who was still living. Wilcox must have been bitterly disappointed when she initially turned down the part. Only after Ingrid Bergman and Michelle Morgan both rejected the role did Wilcox manage to convince Anna to do it.

No matter how good Trevor was in the film – and as usual he was very good – this was meant to be Anna Neagle's picture, and ultimately some critics thought that both she and the film fell short of expectations. Others, however, consider it a classic. I actually find it a difficult film to assess because unlike many films of its era, both British and American, this one doesn't wear well: it was good for 1950 but lacking in any kind of inspired direction to allow it to withstand the years of innovation. On the other hand, Wilcox didn't glamorise his subject, as his American contemporaries might well have done. There is a stark feel to the whole picture, particularly of the sufferings Odette underwent at the hands of her Gestapo torturers, and those scenes remain most vivid in the mind.

For Trevor, there was the added pleasure of having his friend Bernard Lee in the cast, and after a day's filming he and Lee would retire to some French bar or restaurant to kick back their heels. But, as usual, no matter how much he may have had to drink in any one evening, Trevor was back on the set in the morning, on time and stone-cold sober. No matter how small a role or how insignificant a film might be, he was always professional when there was a job to be done. In the case of *Odette* he knew he had a role that had to be treated with respect in a film that was equally deserving of respect. 'The war was still fresh in the memory,' he told me, 'and although dear Anna had the leading role, I was playing someone who was a living hero, so that put a great responsibility on me which was not to be taken lightly. In fact, I got to meet Peter Churchill who stayed with us all through filming.'

Dame Anna Neagle told me:

> We had Odette and Peter Churchill with us all the time, and we spent six weeks going over all the ground they covered during the War before we began filming. Herbert, Trevor and I went to all the spots where Odette and Churchill carried out their work, and we met people who had been in the Gestapo headquarters where Odette was tortured. All those things we saw for ourselves.
>
> All that was invaluable to Trevor Howard and myself. He had tremendous respect for Peter Churchill and wanted to give as honest a portrayal as possible.
>
> You can't fault Trevor. I was very fortunate to be able to work with him in that picture, and with Peter Ustinov, too, who played an important part. I know that Trevor has a certain reputation, but I've worked with other actors who like their beer and whisky, like Errol Flynn, and in Flynn's case he could be absolutely charming when sober but horrible when he'd drunk too much. But Trevor was always charming, and I never saw him drunk as I did Flynn.
>
> Trevor was also very unassuming about his success. He wasn't a film star prima donna. I only wish I'd made more films with him.

Returning to England, Trevor took Helen off to the small village of Arkley in Hertfordshire for a weekend. They immediately fell in love with the place, and now that Trevor was earning a substantial living making movies, they decided to look for a house there. Before the weekend was over, they'd found the cottage where they would spend the rest of their lives together. It became a haven for Trevor, away from the fast and hectic life of film-making. Said Patrick Newell:

> Trevor had two lives. He had a life up in Arkley with Helen, and that was very much a real home life. He had a

fairly lovely sort of rambling house. I remember going into his study once and there were the slippers in front of the TV and the cigarettes and a very warm comfortable armchair.

It struck me as being a very real home, and it wasn't at all like the life he had in the bar or at the studio. It was a different world to all that.

There is a pub in Arkley with a white gate across the road, and there's a field by it and a sort of footpath across it to Trevor's house. It was like Trevor's own path leading to his local pub.

It struck me that he didn't do a lot of entertaining at home. Home was home. He was always saying 'Oh you must come for the weekend,' but people of that era were always saying 'come for the weekend, old boy'. But I don't think anyone ever did, except for business, like film producers and directors and some of his close friends.

It wasn't a sort of open house thing like with a lot of the younger generation of actors always popping in and out all the time of O'Toole's place, or someone like that.

Much of his time during the summer was spent watching cricket, and although he had a thriving career in films he also had one burning ambition, as he explained. 'I've always loved cricket and I was determined to become a playing member of the MCC. Did it as well. Played a number of games, but every now and then a film would come along and interrupt my playing.'

One such film was *The Clouded Yellow* which took him far away from the cricket grounds of Lord's and the Oval to the Lake District. He played a secret service agent demoted to cataloguing butterflies who meets a young girl wrongly accused of murder. In the role of the young girl was 21-year-old Jean Simmons, already a veteran of more than a dozen films who would, at the end of 1950, be voted the fourth biggest attraction – British or American – in British cinema. Under the direction of Ralph Thomas, who began his long and successful association with producer Betty Box on this film, *The Clouded Yellow* proved an engaging thriller – complete with an exciting chase through the Lake District – that many

likened to a Hitchcock film. It was extremely popular with the
audiences.

A little way down in the cast list was an up-and-coming
young actor by the name of Kenneth More. I met him in 1980
on the set of one of his last films, *A Tale Of Two Cities*. He told
me then, 'Dear old Trevor Howard is one of my closest
friends. Only we didn't seem to work together much.' I
mentioned *The Battle Of Britain*, made in 1969, and he said:

> But we never seemed to be in it at the same time. There
> were so many people in that film. We did one picture
> together in the Lake District before I was anything
> important in films really. He was a big star then but we
> seemed to hit it off.
>
> In the evenings he'd say, 'Come on, old man, time for a
> quick one.' And before you knew it you'd had a few
> drinks more than you'd expected.
>
> Then the landlord would call 'Time', and Trevor
> would reply, 'Just one more, Tom or Bill,' or whatever
> the landlord's name was. He's an irresistible man. And if
> you had a day off, he'd say, 'Spot of cricket, old boy?' and
> we'd be out knocking a cricket ball about. I've never
> known anyone so in love with cricket.

When the film was over Trevor returned to Arkley and
allowed himself time to enjoy his home surroundings for a
while, particularly as he could find nothing among the pile of
scripts sent him to get enthusiastic about. He was now in a
position to be more selective, and so he accepted nothing –
until a proposition came from Carol Reed to make *An Outcast
Of The Islands* in Ceylon and Borneo. The script by William
Fairchild from Joseph Conrad's novel wasn't at all bad. And
Carol Reed was, after all, one director he could enjoy a drink
with anywhere. He decided this was a film he should do.

By this time Reed seemed to have become fascinated with
the theme of Englishmen in foreign lands. In some ways it
began with *The Third Man*, although the main character in
that was American, but it was a theme he developed more
fully in *An Outcast Of The Islands* and then continued with his
successive films, *Our Man In Havana*, *The Man Between* and *The
Running Man*.

It must have been a peculiar experience for Trevor returning to Ceylon after so many years. As it turned out, filming this story of a clerk working in the South Seas didn't prove to be the happy experience he had hoped for. It was a particularly difficult picture to make: as Reed struggled to dramatise the complex structure of a man going to seed Trevor fought to overcome some of the weaknesses in the script.

Reed wanted to make what seemed like little more than a routine adventure of smuggling in the South Seas into a study of moral corruption: the clerk becomes involved with smuggling, betrays his employer and finally becomes a broken man. Surprisingly Ralph Richardson turned in a rather hammy performance as a sea captain while the rest of the cast, including Robert Morley, Wendy Hiller and Wilfrid Hyde White, did rather well. But it was Trevor who dominated the picture. He succeeds admirably in retaining attention throughout a film that fell short of expectations, although the photography by John Wilcox is outstanding throughout.

It seems that Trevor went back to Arkley intent on being more careful about any future films, and for a while he turned down offers for any film he felt doubtful about. In 1952 he made only one film, *The Gift Horse*. In it he played a Naval officer who reluctantly takes charge of an old US destroyer given to Britain at the outbreak of World War Two. He was well supported by a cast that included Richard Attenborough, James Donald, Dora Bryan and Bernard Lee, so a few end-of-day high jinks were to be expected. Also in the cast was another renowned drinker, American actor Sonny Tufts, a name that became a joke when, shortly after he made *The Gift Horse*, he was sued by a number of show girls for allegedly biting their thighs! He took to the bottle with a vengeance and became something of a camp figure. Just the mention of his name brought the house down in American nightclubs and on TV.

With fewer films than ever before to get excited about, Trevor was content for the most part to dash off to premières and film festivals when invited, or just to stroll down to the pub, wearing a bit deeper that footpath across the field leading to his local. And during the summer months he would pop down to Lord's to watch a little cricket.

It was at Lord's, in 1952 that Patrick Newell first met Trevor.

I used to go to cricket and I first met Trevor at Lords. I was a member of Middlesex and of course he was a terrific cricketer and as much a fan as Robert Morley and Wilfred Hyde White were with race horses.

I used to go to the pavilion as a young man and sit around there, and he was always there. At the time I was a student at RADA, and I looked at Trevor and idolised this big star. And as time went on we got onto nodding terms. He was nodding at everyone because he knew everyone and everybody there knew him. He didn't talk a lot about show business, it was always cricket.

Then I did a television play – quite a good one – and Trevor came over to me and said, 'I saw you on the telly. I didn't know you were an actor.'

And I said, 'Well, I'm just a starter,' and that was something else we could talk about. Then we got to the stage where he said, 'Are you going to be here on Wednesday?' and I said, 'Yes, probably,' and he said, '*I'll* be, amigo. We'll have a pint.'

So I often used to meet him there and have a drink. But I used to go home while he'd sit there to the very end of the match.

Films annoyed him enormously if he had to go off and make one during a test match. There are stories about Trevor saying 'Yes, I'll make the film but I've got to have these days off.'

'Why?' they'd ask.

'Test match, amigo.'

And apparently in those days they wore it. I think because he was so very good and in demand they shot around him. Well, that was the story. Whether it was true or not, I don't know. I never asked.

Well, apparently it was true, or at least, Harry Andrews thought so. He said that Trevor had it written into his contract that he didn't have to work if there was a test match on.

Around that time he wasn't working much anyway as he continued to reject the film offers put to him. Then, in 1953, he finally returned to the stage to star in *The Devil's General* by Carl Zuckmayer. It opened at the Edinburgh Festival and then toured the country successfully before coming to the Savoy in London.

His co-star was a man he greatly admired, Wilfrid Lawson, a great character and a marvellous actor who had made films on both sides of the Atlantic. He'd even co-starred twice with John Wayne. Only 53 at the time, Lawson's drinking had taken a heavy toll on his years and had also earned him a bad reputation in the theatre. He only got the part in *The Devil's General* because Trevor had insisted the producers hire him. Such was the clout that Trevor Howard carried in those days. How many actors could insist on a 'bad risk' co-star and get days off to watch test matches too?

5

The Howard Roar

'I'VE NEVER RAISED hell, amigo. I just like to enjoy myself, that's all,' Trevor told me. So I asked him about the stories that he and Peter Finch were hellraising drinking buddies back in the Fifties.

'That was all Press crap. I only made one film with Finchie, but he was always a somewhat secretive man. I hardly knew him.'

The film was *The Heart Of The Matter*, made at Shepperton Studios and on location in Sierra Leone. It was a Graham Greene story, set in 1942. A South African police commissioner, played by Trevor, has a torrid love affair with a girl (Maria Schell) while his wife is away. His Catholic background and the threat of blackmail lead him to the point of mental breakdown.

Peter Finch appeared relatively briefly but not without impact as a Catholic priest who comes to the commissioner to try and give him some peace of mind. It was a tricky scene since the director George More O'Ferrall always felt that the good priest would have attempted to produce a reason to enable him to give the commissioner absolution. When he told Greene this, he had the impression that Greene didn't mind if he rewrote the scene. So O'Ferrall, Finchie and Trevor found themselves working with a Jesuit theologian to try and reshape the scene. When Greene saw the results he wasn't pleased, so O'Ferrall had Trevor and Finchie back in the studio to reshoot the scene the way Greene wrote it. This must have been particularly frustrating for the actors who had worked so hard to get it the way they agreed it should be. Perhaps if they had been dealing with a lesser writer, Trevor might have been able to use his now considerable status to fight to keep the change. But then again, as he told me, 'I never push my weight around on a film, old boy. Not like

some of those actors who think they're the whole bloody film.'
'Would you include Brando in that class?' I asked.
He replied:

> You could say that, I have raised my voice a couple of
> times in protest when I thought it was really needed.
> Once was when I was in *Sons And Lovers* . . . Another time
> was when the producer of *The Heart Of The Matter* decided
> they could do without me on location. I was told, 'You
> don't have to go, old boy. We can use a double in long
> shots and just film you in the studio.' Well, that made me
> angry and I told them that if I was paid to do a film, I
> was going to do it properly, and I convinced them to let
> me go to Sierra Leone.

It would appear that all the hassle was worth the end result:
The Heart Of The Matter was always one of Trevor's own
personal favourites, and he received some excellent notices.
Time Magazine wrote: 'Trevor Howard as Scobie is pity in the
flesh; and moreover, a spectator gets the sense that he is not
one aspect in one scene, and another in another, but the whole
man at every moment.' The *Daily Mail* said: 'Trevor Howard,
whose work seems to mature and expand with every
performance, gives a magnificent study of a nice man tortured
by the consequences of weakness he can recognise but not
overcome.'

At the time the film was made, Peter Finch was renowned,
even at that early stage of his career, as a devoted drinker.
Since he and Trevor, whose reputation was just as awesome,
were working together, some reporter decided they must also
be drinking together. The story came out that here were two
hellraising drinking buddies. And the story may have had a
grain of truth in it if it weren't for two things. The first is that
no matter who I've talked to, they have all categorically
stated, without my asking, that Trevor was never a hellraiser.
And the second is that it would seem that despite their mutual
fondness for the bottle, there was very little communal drinking
between them. Away from the set Trevor saw little of Finchie,
and once the film was over he saw hardly anything of him.
Finch seemed to prefer to keep himself to himself, and even

when he lived just down the road from Trevor, Finch never stopped by just to say hello.

However, he obviously admired Trevor enormously because when his wife gave birth to a boy, Finch named him Howard Charles Finch.

For a while Trevor seemed to enjoy the tag of hellraiser, seeing it all as one big joke. But I think he expected it to fade and in his latter years he seemed positively irritated by the description. He defined his attitude to enjoying life in his own way very well when he told Terence Pettigrew, 'I don't raise hell, old boy. I prefer to creep off into a corner and talk to no one. But it's true I do enjoy myself. Possibly more than the average chap. That's to be expected after a hard film.'

If Trevor didn't raise hell, he certainly raised the roof quite a bit. Patrick Newell said, 'He was famous for his "roar", The Trevor Howard Roar! He used to come through the doors of a restaurant with a loud "Whoooaaa!" Mainly in small Greek restaurants in the Fulham Road.' And Harry Andrews said, 'When he'd had a few drinks he could be noisy. If he was really pissed he was a roarer.'

No wonder Trevor himself called that decade 'The Roaring Fifties'.

Venice was soon to reverberate with the famous 'roar'. In 1953 Trevor went there to make *The Stranger's Hand*, another Graham Greene story. Although produced by British Lion, it was in many other ways an Italian film, directed by Mario Soldati, photographed by Enzo Serafin and with music by Nino Rota. The role of the British espionage officer who goes to meet his son in Venice and is kidnapped by enemy agents was tailor-made for Trevor. But the film hardly stretched him as an actor, nor was it, even from the outset, likely to succeed commercially.

With good scripts becoming seemingly more rare, he decided that year, 1953, to take off for America, where he still wasn't particularly well known, to appear in a live television play, *Still Life*. This original one-act play by Noel Coward, which had been filmed as *Brief Encounter*, was just one in a number of plays in the TV series *Noel Coward's Tonight at 8.30*. Trevor found himself teamed up with Ginger Rogers in the

Celia Johnson role while behind the camera was famed Hollywood ogre Otto Preminger. Preminger had the reputation for being the director most hated by actors, and Trevor didn't like him. But he found the experience of performing live for the camera stimulating, with almost the same kind of edge that comes with performing in the theatre – except that the audience isn't visible. The play was recorded in New York where Trevor took the opportunity to seek out some of the old jazz clubs he'd visited when he was just 15, as well as visiting the newer ones.

From 1953 onwards Trevor often starred in American TV plays and films, and much of it he considered to be among his finest work. But he always had one huge disappointment: 'None of it ever gets shown in Britain, which is a damn shame. Good stuff some of it.'

Still unable to find a film he liked, he returned to America in 1954 to do *The Flower Of Pride* on television. It was directed by Frank Schaffner, one of the most successful TV directors, who won three Emmys for his work on the small screen before proving himself equally successful on the big screen with films like *Planet Of The Apes* and *Patton*.

Trevor followed this with another Stateside TV play, *Deception*, before returning to England for the enjoyable experience of being directed by John Gielgud at the Lyric Theatre, Hammersmith, in Chekhov's *The Cherry Orchard*. Gielgud had directed a number of plays by this time, and actors liked working for him because, being an actor, he understood their problems and was more sympathetic than most non-acting directors. Sir John never considered himself an innovative director: his interpretations of plays were straightforward and he didn't spend hours explaining to a confused cast what he was aiming for.

Like Harry Andrews, and a good many other actors, Sir John Gielgud was disappointed that Trevor never pursued his theatrical career with the kind of impetus that could have made him one of the truly great names of British theatre. Said Sir John:

I loved working with him when he gave a brilliant performance in the part of Lopahin in *The Cherry Orchard* at the Lyric. But the discipline of eight times a week seemed to be too much for him, and to my very great sorrow he left the cast after only about five weeks. He once played Petruchio in *The Taming Of The Shrew* in Edinburgh with Patricia Burke, but he left the cast before the production came to London. I don't think he did any other classical work.

I remember seeing him in Rattigan's *French Without Tears*, playing a very small part very early in his career. Except for *Brief Encounter*, he seldom seemed to be offered parts really worthy of his talent, but he contributed notably to any part that seemed to come his way.

Trevor must have felt in something of a rut. He was unable to sustain enough interest in any stage part to make his career in the theatre progress any further, and from then on his stage appearances became fewer and further between. As for films, there just didn't seem to be any around that excited him enough to accept any offers. What he did do, whenever the opportunity arose, was to take off to any part of the world where he was invited by film festival organisers to be a guest at their star-studded events.

'I love travelling,' he said. 'Not every film takes me off to wonderful places so I have always gone to any film festivals or premières I get asked to. It's a wonderful way to see the world. Yes, it's a privilege, I can't complain at all.'

At this time, in 1954, whether out of desperation just to work, or simply to see Paris, he accepted an offer from a French producer to appear in *The Lovers Of Lisbon*. This time he was not to be the star and had to take third billing. It was a confused plot in which he played a Scotland Yard police inspector on the trail of a rich woman who has killed her husband and takes up with a man who has just been acquitted of the murder of his wife who . . . ! Well, he must have gone into it knowing he'd get little out of it other than a free trip to France.

What he really needed now to keep his film career from floundering was an undisputed hit. That's when he got a call from producer Irving Allen to come to Hollywood for a couple of days to negotiate with actor/director José Ferrer who wanted Trevor to star in his war picture, *Cockleshell Heroes*.

Trevor didn't waste time in flying out to America. This was an opportunity for him to make his first American movie and a chance to achieve true international film stardom. He accepted the film and flew back to celebrate with Helen.

José Ferrer, a versatile actor from Puerto Rico, had a considerable reputation on Broadway where he had directed and acted, and also enjoyed film star status since making his film début in *Joan Of Arc* in 1948. In 1950 he confirmed his place in Hollywood history when he gave his Oscar-winning performance as *Cyrano de Bergerac*. In 1955 he directed his first film, *The Shrike*, which he also starred in, and Columbia Pictures and Irving Allen's own Warwick Pictures felt confident enough of Ferrer's talent to join forces to give him his next directorial effort, *Cockleshell Heroes*, an expensive war picture in which he would also star. His fee for the double assignment was the dollar equivalent of £50,000.

The screenplay by Bryan Forbes and Richard Maibaum followed the exploits of 10 marines as they went through training for a special mission to canoe their way into Bordeaux harbour and mine German shipping. Like *The Way Ahead*, it began with typical barrack-room humour and culminated in tragedy and drama. Said Trevor, 'The best thing about *Cockleshell Heroes* was filming in Portugal. Beautiful country. While I was there I ended up doing the commentary for a documentary about the country which won more awards than the film ever did. I went all over the world promoting the documentary. As for the film – well.'

Well – what Trevor didn't say was that José Ferrer directed and José Ferrer starred and in the process didn't make himself too popular with Irving Allen. At the time Allen said, 'When Ferrer finished the film, we found that he had made a *tour de force* for José Ferrer. He seems to have forgotten about the rest of the cast. I've been doing close-ups of Trevor Howard that Joe forgot to do.'

The film, however, was a huge success and, despite its predictability, not a bad film at all. Whatever one might say about José Ferrer, he has talent which is evident in the picture, both behind and in front of the camera. But not even by trying to leave out Trevor's close-ups could Ferrer expect anything other than to be acted off the screen by him, as all the critics agreed.

6

An Award-Winning Event

THE DOCUMENTARY THAT Trevor had made in Portugal was called *April In Portugal*. It gave him the holiday of a life-time as he dashed around the world, visiting 12 countries. Helen went with him and they ended up in Switzerland for their own private vacation.

Returning to England, he received an offer that, if nothing else, confirmed his international film star status. He was asked to appear in a cameo role in Michael Todd's spectacular Todd-AO production *Around The World In Eighty Days*. He knew this was no mere bit part but a true 'star' cameo: the list of other cameos included Frank Sinatra, Marlene Dietrich, Charles Boyer, Noel Coward and Ronald Colman – all of them big star names. And he was among them.

The main star of the film was David Niven as Phileas Fogg, while other major roles were played by Robert Newton, Fernandel and Shirley MacLaine. Trevor, like all the star guests, was paid about £5,000 for about 15 minutes' screen time.

Around that time, in 1955, Trevor was one of a number of eminent British actors approached to play the part of Professor Higgins in the new stage musical *My Fair Lady*. Trevor had only sung once before on the stage, in *The Recruiting Officer*, and he didn't feel he could carry it off again in a major musical. It also promised to be a long running success, and he couldn't face the thought of going through the same performance several times a week for more than a few weeks. The role went to his friend since their days together in *French Without Tears*, Rex Harrison, who became the definitive

Prof. Higgins in both the stage and screen versions of *My Fair Lady*.

While Michael Todd, David Niven and director Michael Anderson were still shooting *Around The World In Eighty Days* in around 180 days (or thereabouts), Trevor went off to Mexico for his second major Hollywood film (or third if you count *Around The World*), *Run For The Sun*. Although produced by an American, Harry Tatelman, it was directed by Roy Boulting, one of the famous Boulting Brothers from England. This was Roy's first American picture. He usually worked in partnership with brother John who produced while Roy directed, and their early collaborative work – mainly typical British film-market stuff – was held in high regard by the critics. *Run For The Sun* gave Roy a chance to show he could produce work with international appeal, and he worked closely with Dudley Nichols (one of John Ford's favourite screenwriters) on the screenplay.

Based on a 1932 movie, *The Most Dangerous Game* (which was also remade in 1945 as *A Game Of Death*) *Run For The Sun* told of an American author and a female journalist crashlanding in the Mexican jungle and stumbling onto a plantation run by the mysterious Lord Haw-Haw (in the original film he was Count Zaroff) and his band of Nazi renegades.

Trevor had the role of the sadistic Lord, and for once proved thoroughly unlikeable in a chillingly convincing performance. It was also a role that virtually wiped out his chance ever to become a convincing major heroic film star and established him more as a screen character actor. Although there would be the occasional typical 'leading man' role, it was being a successful and unintentional scene-stealing character actor that kept him solidly in work for the rest of his life.

Harry Tatelman had wanted Leo Genn to play the part of Lord Haw-Haw but when Genn read the script he turned it down flat. The name Trevor Howard meant little to Tatelman, but to Roy Boulting it was a name to be respected, and so he prompted his producer to offer the role to Trevor. It meant taking third billing, but Trevor was excited by the prospect of further exposure to American audiences and, no doubt, of working for the first time in Mexico – and most likely trying out the tequila. Richard Widmark had top billing as the author, while second billing went to Jane Greer who had actually retired from the screen in 1953 to raise a family. *Run For The Sun* was a temporary come-back for her, and Trevor found her far more amiable than Widmark who could at times by a little difficult although a thoroughly professional and extremely gifted actor. He enjoyed all the trimmings of being a Hollywood star and didn't seem at all bothered that Trevor hadn't even been given his own dressing room as he and Jane Greer had.

Trevor once told Patrick Newell how Jane Greer came to his rescue by going to the producer and giving him a piece of her mind for not treating Trevor on an equal footing with Widmark and herself. To Tatelman, Trevor was just some relatively unknown English actor who was filling in for a part he'd wanted Leo Genn to play. But thanks to her Trevor was given a dressing room of his own.

During production a rumour began to circulate that Trevor was having an affair with Jane Greer's stand-in. She was the kind of girl who had no pretensions about wanting to be a star and had a lively sense of humour that appealed to Trevor. They did get on extremely well, but this time Helen shrugged off the stories, and when she met the girl, the two became firm friends.

Not far from their location, Robert Mitchum was shooting *Bandido*. Almost as soon as Mitchum and Trevor met they hit it off, especially as they both enjoyed a drink in the hotel bar at the end of the day. In time they would get to work together in two movies, establishing an even closer friendship and a mutual admiration that was rare for Trevor because there were actually very few big Hollywood stars he ever really liked.

Work-wise, Trevor was inactive for the rest of 1956, His last three pictures had earned him enough to be able to sit back and reject all the abysmal scripts that were sent to him. For a while he considered doing *Omar Khayam*, an Arabian Nights fantasy about a Persian poet defending the Shah from assassins. Cornel Wilde was slotted to play the hero and Trevor should have been the Shah. But the screenplay was poor and he immediately saw all the warning lights: this was just going to be a costume pantomime. He wisely dropped out and Michael Rennie did it instead.

It now seemed certain that Trevor was no longer considered a suitable leading man. The only lead parts he was offered were hardly complemented by the poor scripts he had to plough through, while everything else promised little more than supporting character parts in films that he didn't feel would amount to much.

Finally, in 1957, he reluctantly gave in and did *Interpol* for Irving Allen and Albert R. Broccoli (who was only a few years away from hitting the jackpot with the James Bond movies). At least it offered locations in Rome and Genoa as well as in Britain. The real star of the film was beefy Victor Mature, who was perhaps more suited to his musclemen roles in historical and biblical films than this dreary crime stuff, playing a US Anti-Narcotics agent trailing across Europe in an attempt to smash a dope-smuggling organisation. Billed above Trevor, too, was Anita Ekberg, the statuesque, voluptuous former Miss Sweden who'd been in one good film (*War and Peace*) and several moderate-to-lousy pictures. Trevor's only comment on the film was, 'I thought there was something more worthwhile in life than acting with an ex-beauty queen.'

But while the critics derided the film and the two major stars, Trevor could console himself with the fact that at least the critics didn't deride him as well. *Picturegoer*, for instance, said his acting 'made [Mature and Ekberg] look slightly silly,' and Leslie Halliwell in his brief review in his *Film Guide* thought the film was 'electrified by one performance [Howard's].'

Next came something he felt could turn out to be worthwhile, which also gave him a stab at playing a lead role again. In *Manuela* he played a captain of a tramp steamer who finds a half-caste girl on his boat, smuggled on by the steamer's chief engineer. Furious at first, the Captain gradually falls in love with her. The film was a sensitive portrait of a middle-aged man's infatuation with a much younger woman, played quite well by Italian Elsa Martinelli who had been discovered only two years earlier by Kirk

Douglas for his own production, *The Indian Fighter*. Director Guy Hamilton captured a down-beat atmosphere, and Trevor came away from it not only having had the pleasure of working in Spain, but also with some superb personal notices to add to his collection of press cuttings. Noted critic Dilys Powell said: 'Perhaps it is only the depth and subtlety of Trevor Howard's playing which makes one conscious of a lack in his partner . . . I can think of no actor like (him) for suggesting the heartbreak behind the bleak, the unwavering look.' And the *Evening Standard*'s Philip Oakes said: 'Trevor Howard gives the film an extra dimension with his painfully precise portrait of the anguished old man of the sea. This is a great performance.'

That year, 1957, at the invitation of the film's director Otto Preminger, Trevor and Helen went off to Paris for the première of *St Joan* at the Paris Opera House. Although Trevor hadn't liked Preminger when they had worked together on American TV, it was nevertheless an invitation he had accepted, since he enjoyed premières, especially if they were abroad. At the première also were Jack Hawkins and his wife Doreen, and Kenneth More and his wife who was always known as Bill! They were to represent the British film community. Also in attendance were the stars of the film, Jean Seberg and Richard Widmark, and the French President.

Trevor and the British party were given a special box at the Opera House in which only three people could sit in each row. So the wives sat in the front row and the husbands at the back. Shortly after the film began, the three British actors made up their minds that it was going to be almost two hours of sheer unadulterated boredom. Kenneth More whispered to Jack Hawkins, 'Let's slip out for a drink at the Café de L'Opéra. No one will know we've gone.' Jack didn't think it ethical and so they remained a while longer, enduring the agonies of a film that was destined for failure, until Trevor said, 'I can't stand it any longer. Let's get out of here.'

Without a word to their wives, they crept out and managed to escape unseen to the café across the road. They sat outside knocking back whiskeys until a man approached them. He turned out to be an English reporter and he asked them why they weren't at the première. 'Kenny fainted,' piped up Trevor, 'and we had to carry him out for some fresh air.' They returned to their box in time to catch the end of the film and without their wives ever knowing they'd been gone. But the next day they read the reporter's account of how the three of them had sneaked out of the premiere. When Preminger read the report he was furious and vowed that none of them would ever work with him again. That didn't bother Trevor in the least. He had no intention of ever working with him again, anyway.

But one director he did want to work with again was his friend Carol Reed, and he did so towards the end of 1957 in *The Key*. He played the commander of a sea-going tug during World War Two, who passes on the key of an apartment to his friend in case he is killed. With the apartment goes a beautiful woman. When he does die, his successor also has the key duplicated knowing that his life is constantly on the line.

It was all very symbolic with supernatural overtones, a touch of romance and a helping of action, all of which never quite gells. Since Trevor's character is killed off quite early in the film, it is William Holden, the inheritor of the key, who takes centre stage, along with Sophia Loren as the woman who owns the apartment.

Although it failed to be a thought-provoking prestige picture, it was a happy experience for Trevor, who once more found his friend Bernie Lee a bit further down in the cast list.

'If William Holden is to be believed,' said Patrick Newell, 'when Trevor and Bernie and Carol Reed made *The Key*, it was something to be seen. I gather it was quite an event.'

The event only became something to be seen though after a day's filming. During the day it was hard work with all concentration focused on making what they had all hoped would be a superior film. But in the evening it was down to the studio bar where William Holden (who had a reputation for liking his booze) would have joined them. According to Patrick, William Holden was one of the few American actors Trevor liked, even though the Hollywood star system forbade Trevor from travelling in the same car as Holden who, since the phenomenal success of *The Bridge On The River Kwai*, had become a very rich and important star.

But Trevor must have been irritated by Sophia Loren's method of acting. She virtually walked through rehearsals, saying her lines with very little conviction, always saving her performance for actual 'takes'. She was aware that the men in the cast found this odd and unnerving but it was her way of working, and Carol Reed indulged her in this. But she gave the actors nothing in the way of chemistry until the cameras rolled. Despite the problems, and the fact that Trevor's role was relatively brief, the critics were once again unanimous in their estimation that he stole all the acting honours. And the British Film Academy agreed, awarding him their Best Actor Award for 1958.

7

African Adventure

ROMAIN GARY'S BOOK, *The Roots Of Heaven*, had won the coveted Prix Goncourt in France. It told the story of Morel, driven by a frantic desire to stop the slaughter of elephants before the great herds become extinct.

Trevor's love for elephants made this a story that especially appealed to him, and when in 1958 he heard that mogul Darryl F. Zanuck had bought the rights to film the book, he asked his agent to make an approach to Zanuck for the role of Morel. But Zanuck didn't want him. Apparently he preferred to have an American star name and Trevor just didn't fit the bill.

Meanwhile, preparations for the filming went ahead. Director John Huston had also been keen to make the film version, and had asked his studio, 20th-Century Fox, to buy it for him. Then he learned that Zanuck, chief of production at Fox since 1933 and now wanting to produce his own films, had exercised his right with the studio to pick his own subject every two years. They had secured the rights of *The Roots Of Heaven* for him.

Huston was desperate to make the picture. He negotiated with Zanuck and got the job of directing. They set about selecting a cast, William Holden was the American star that Zanuck was after for Morel. Other actors chosen included Juliette Greco, Eddie Albert, Orson Welles and, in his penultimate role, Errol Flynn.

By this time Flynn's body had deteriorated to such a point through drugs and drink that Jack Warner described him as 'the living dead.' Aged only 49, and with just one year left to live, he wasn't even a pale imitation of his former handsome, debonair self. Yet he was still an irresistible rascal with lashings of charm and wit who didn't give a damn what anybody else thought. He was also a man with a great sense of charity, as Trevor was to discover.

Flynn's role was that of a broken ex-Army Major, a rogue who redeems himself by joining forces with Morel to stop the extermination of the elephants. Since Flynn was by nature a conservationist, it was a role he believed in. And, since Huston knew Flynn had his limitations as an actor, the role was tailored to suit them.

It was decided that the cast and crew would gather in Paris and thence head for Africa with the vast unit of American, French, English and Italian technicians and set-workers to shoot the bulk of the film. They would then return to France where Orson Welles, who wasn't needed on location, could do his scenes at the Boulogne Studios.

But by the time everyone was in Paris, William Holden had dropped out and a new Morel was being sought. So Trevor wasted no time in taking Helen off to Paris for an unscheduled holiday, ensuring that he met John Huston in the process. The outcome was that Trevor got the part and went off to French Equatorial Africa with the rest of the unit in January.

The location was hellish: the heat proved so intense that it was impossible to maintain any kind of consistent shooting schedule. Filming usually began at dawn and continued until noon and then the film stock had to be stored in iced containers. The temperature often reached 130° and the humidity was severe. Everyone lived in tents and mud huts, sleeping under mosquito nets. Flynn shared his with his 15-year-old girlfriend, Beverly. While many of the cast and crew were dropping like the flies that crawled all over the food and in everybody's hair, Errol Flynn somehow managed to remain relatively untouched by the illnesses that were rife. Trevor recalled how awful everybody looked as they endured the atrocious and uncivilised conditions, while Flynn would emerge from his tent impeccably dressed in jungle uniform.

Flynn's explanation for surviving this hellish location was, 'I've been through the jungles of New Guinea. They were enough to prepare me for anything. Also, I refuse to drink water on location, sticking with vodka and fruit juice – which no doubt helps!' He should have passed on his tip to everyone else. Eddie Albert collapsed with sunstroke while taking photographs on a mountain slope and became delirious for a while. One of the crew neglected to take his anti-malaria pills and contracted the most virulent form of malaria and died. Zanuck's son-in-law Bobby Jacks came down with the same form of malaria but survived. There was a total of 960 cases for the medical team to deal with, including gonorrhoea, and the unit decreased in numbers as actors and technicians were sent back home to recover.

Flynn had his own food flown in from Paris but Trevor and the rest of the cast and unit made do with the meals supplied on location. During a meal served up by the film unit's caterers, Huston noticed a peculiar flavour to the meat. 'It tasted too sweet and fresh to be flown in from so-called civilisation,' he said. 'After making a few enquiries we found that some of our natives were selling our canteen chef human bodies they'd killed on warring raids.'

Different locations required different forms of accommodation and at one time Juliette Greco, the half-Corsican, half-French actress, found herself sharing a huge hut with a number of men. She said, 'In morning these men are waking up, some very nicely, some not so nicely. Mr Trevor Howard always waking up nice, but Mr Huston not always waking up so nice.'

And the fact that Mr Trevor Howard was 'always waking up nice' wasn't because he'd been abstaining from alcoholic beverages the evening before while in the company of Errol Flynn. He struck a tremendous rapport with Flynn. According to Patrick Newell:

He absolutely worshipped Errol Flynn. I don't think many people ever realised that his biggest hero of all time was Flynn. I sat one night at Pinewood Studios with Trevor when we were doing *The Long Duel*, and I can remember sitting all night through until make-up call the next day while he spoke about Errol Flynn the entire time. Not hellraising stories. Just amazing stories.

They became great friends and when they did that film in Africa they had a 15-cwt truck behind them absolutely full of whisky that followed them everywhere they went. I never heard Trevor say, 'God, we got really drunk there.' Never. He used to say, 'We had a couple of jars on that one.' Always the understatement.

Flynn owned an island and he used to come in on his yacht, dressed up in white trousers and peak cap, and the whole island would line up to greet him. Flynn had virtually bought them but he made sure that they had hospitals and everything they needed. He kept the whole place. And that appealed to Trevor very much. He kept saying, 'A real gentleman, old boy. A real gentleman.'

Flynn was a great joker and Trevor was happy to join in with his pranks. On location Flynn formed a club called The Roisterers with himself as president and Trevor as his deputy, and their one aim in life was to expound on the greatness of W.C. Fields and, in particular, of John Barrymore who was Flynn's own hero. Needless to say, not too many people joined their club, but they had fun doing it, like a couple of schoolboys playing a game.

Flynn played one joke that Trevor knew nothing about: just before they were set to return to Paris, he sent a letter to Romain Gary who had adapted the screenplay (with Patrick Leigh-Fermor) saying, 'What the hell is this damned film supposed to be all about anyway?' He signed it, 'Trevor Howard'.

Throughout filming Huston had been battling against time and the elements which were forecast to change from intense heat to torrential rain. The African rain seasons were to be avoided at all costs as roads would become impassable and evacuation extremely difficult if not impossible. 'We barely made it,' recalled Trevor. 'Huston got us out of there just half a day ahead of the rains. Twelve more hours in Africa and we might all be there yet.'

Arriving in France at the beginning of May, still more members of the production were stricken down with after-effects of the African location. Flynn came down with a mild case of malaria and Darryl F. Zanuck, who had remained perfectly fit throughout the location, was struck with shingles. Juliette Greco had unknowingly contracted a rare disease of the blood and her blood pressure had fallen dangerously low, so she had to be quickly hospitalised. Huston emerged from it all in perfect health, as did Trevor.

But while he may have had a tremendous adventure

throughout, as an actor Trevor had problems in dealing with an inadequate script: there were many passages of weak dialogue which had to be polished up, and the character of Morel was not adequately defined.

Filming continued at the Boulogne Studios and the final scenes were shot in the forest at Fontainebleau on the outskirts of Paris. The budget came in at a staggering $4,300,000.

Again, as is no surprise, Trevor's performance was considered the outstanding feature in what was another disappointing picture, the blame for which must rest with Huston. When once asked for his personal assessment of Trevor Howard, John Huston, said, 'Magnificent. There is one of the greatest actors in the world. He has much in common with the late Humphrey Bogart, you know, although Howard is the greater virtuoso. How superbly he would have handled Bogie's part in *The African Queen.*'

As for Flynn, he pretty much played himself, which was all anyone expected and hoped for, but all too often he looked bloated and much older than he was.

His own African adventure finally over, Trevor spent time in America on a promotional tour for the film and took time out to frequent many of New York's jazz joints. Then he was whisked off, not involuntarily, to Australia to promote *The Key*: the Australian test matches were being played and Trevor had every intention of catching as much cricket as he could while there.

Then along came a film he decided to make and he interrupted his cricket and he flew home. *Moment Of Danger*, with Edmund Purdom and the tragic Dorothy Dandridge, was a crime thriller about thieves pursuing each other to Malaga. Trevor must have gone into it with his eyes open, knowing it would never be a particularly good picture, but he wanted to work. It was the last film Dorothy Dandridge made. Six years later, in 1965, she was found dead, apparently from an overdose of barbiturates. However, there is some conflicting evidence that in some ways makes her death almost as mysterious as Monroe's. Dandridge was the first real black sex symbol and most immediately remembered for two Otto Preminger musicals, *Carmen Jones* and *Porgy And Bess*.

I asked Trevor if, while making *Moment Of Danger*, he had been aware of the more destructive elements in her life that was to end so soon.

I can't say I really knew too much about her – not from anything she told me anyway. She seemed to have a number of different men in her life from time to time. I suppose like all of us, she needed to be loved but she never really found it.

I can't say that on the set of *Moment Of Danger* she behaved any differently from any other actress. She was late sometimes and I think she liked a drink. There was one particular man around a lot – her manager [Earl Mills] who seemed to be the one man who really cared for her and, I believe, loved her.

But so much of all that was typical of Hollywood. It's always seemed such a destructive place – or maybe it just attracts destructive people. I don't know, old boy.

What was odd at the time was working with a very beautiful, very important black actress who was obviously black but in the film no one ever knew what her nationality was supposed to be. It was taboo, I suppose, because there was she and there was I, a white man, and we were supposed to kiss and just that caused all sorts of trouble. Perhaps that's all part of what finally destroyed her. She must have suffered from racism and the only man she was allowed to kiss on screen was Harry Belafonte. I suppose if you want to be an actor and you're told, 'You can't do this or that because you're black,' that itself is going to destroy you somewhat, don't you think?

Moment Of Danger didn't put any stars in Trevor's crown, but his next film did. In 1960 he went off to Yorkshire to give what would prove to be one of his most outstanding performances in D.H. Lawrence's *Sons And Lovers*. The film was a compelling adaptation of Lawrence's autobiographical novel, dealing with his attempts to escape the prospect of a life in the mines and to make something of his creative talents. Dean Stockwell, an American, was surprisingly effective as the young Lawrence character, egged on by his mother (Wendy Hiller) to make something of his life away from the mines and his drunken bully of a father, played by Trevor Howard. It was a picture full of splendid performances, an intelligent script by Gavin Lambert and T.E.B. Clarke, and the outstanding camera work of Freddie Francis, all neatly packaged by director Jack Cardiff. Cardiff had initially made his name as one of Britain's foremost cinematographers who turned to directing in 1958. *Sons And Lovers* was only his third and probably the most successful of his films as director.

But it was also a film of some tribulation, as Jack Cardiff explained to me when I met him directing photography on the set of *The Awakening*.

Sons And Lovers was a film which had a lot of good things in it, particularly Trevor Howard as the father, and I was very fond of Lawrence and the whole scene. And it was a very successful movie, and there was something about it that obviously made me enjoy doing it.

What marred it in production, not in the final result, but during the time we were making it, was that there were two producers who worked for 20th-Century Fox. There was Jerry Wald in Hollywood and a man called Bob Goldstein who was like Fox's man in London.

First of all they didn't want Trevor Howard at all. Now I have absolutely no idea why, except that they already had a young American actor (Dean Stockwell) playing the Lawrence character, and he was actually very good, and I suppose they may have wanted someone who was more of a star than a first-class actor to play his father. But there was no doubt in my mind that Trevor was perfect for the role, and so we had to get all that sorted out.

While we were shooting up in the real mines that had to be reopened, the two producers seemed to be in competition for control of the picture. The sad thing about it all is that one of them was in America the whole time and the other, as far as I can recall, never saw a foot of film being shot, and all he wanted to do was bring the film in under budget and kept ordering certain scenes to be cut from the schedule. And Wald in Hollywood kept saying to keep the scenes in.

Film-making is always a difficult collaborative work and we were fortunate to have Trevor Howard and Wendy Hiller on the picture because they were not only in support of the work I was trying to do but they were so effective in their roles. That was where a lot of the pleasure was for me, as well as the fact that we were able to work in the mine where Lawrence's father actually worked, and we often ran into people who knew the characters from the book. One extra came up and said 'I'm Miriam's uncle', and another girl came up and said, 'I'm Mrs Doors' daughter'. And it was startling to meet people who were related to characters out of a book who actually existed, although they were called different names.

Trevor remembers the film as being one of the very few in which he found himself forced to push his weight around a bit. He told me:

I nearly walked out on that one because some bloody fool who was supposed to be the producer wanted to cut out some vital scenes just to save money, and we thought it was all getting so ridiculous that Wendy Hiller and myself decided that if the scenes weren't replaced we would quit. It's not the sort of thing I would ever expect from anyone let alone myself, but the film would have suffered and our work would have suffered when it wasn't necessary. Then the office in Hollywood heard about it and probably thought it was blackmail, which I suppose it was, and we got our scenes back. Poor Jack was caught in the middle. We didn't want to let him down because he was fighting to make the film as it should be done. I think in the end we did the right thing. It's not that we were prima donnas or anything like that. I hate it when actors use their weight just so they can be the star. In our case, it was the principle, amigo. The principle. Anyway, I don't think we would have actually quit. Although we were so mad we thought at the time we would.

By and large the critics seemed to be evenly split between

rating the film as a successful attempt and an-almost-successful try. One critic described it as 'an album of decent Edwardian snapshots'. Certainly the acting couldn't be faulted, particularly that of Wendy Hiller, but, as usual, it was Trevor who generally garnered the greatest praise. *Variety*, the American entertainment trade paper and show business bible, wrote: 'Easily the outstanding feature of the production is the powerful performance by Trevor Howard. Always a splendid performer, Howard has rarely been better, giving a moving and wholly believable study of a man equally capable of tenderness and being tough.'

All the efforts to overcome the difficulties imposed throughout production must have seemed worthwhile in retrospect: not only was the picture a great commercial success, but it went on to earn six Oscar nominations – Trevor Howard for Best Actor, Mary Ure for Best Supporting Actress, Jack Cardiff for Best Direction, Freddie Francis for Best Cinematography, Gavin Lambert and T.E.B. Clarke for Best Screenplay, and a Best Picture nomination. However, only Freddie Francis actually walked away with an Oscar in his hand. If the film hadn't been in competition with so much Hollywood-made product it might have faired better. It should have faired better. In any event, the fact that it had received so many nominations added to its prestige, and for Trevor it held up the promise of an exciting decade ahead in important American movies. He was suddenly in demand and he was all set to star in a multi-million dollar picture that had everything going for it – *Mutiny On The Bounty*.

8
Trouble In Tahiti

AT A TIME when huge spectacular block-busters like *The Ten Commandments* and *Ben-Hur* were setting the box office tills ringing all around the world, every major studio wanted to jump on the bandwagon and make their own epic. It all seemed good sound commercial sense, but artistically and creatively what they didn't seem to realise was that because of the extraordinary elements that go into making an epic film they are the easiest films to make badly and the most difficult to make well. The fact that such films usually ran for around three hours – twice as long as the average film – meant that it took at least twice as long to make, and six to nine months making one film can be a great strain on patience and creativity. This isn't helped by the necessity to control crowds of up to several thousand extras, itself taking extra time, especially if they are involved in the usual obligatory battle scenes. Then, if the film is to be based on historical fact, there are usually a great number of characters that have to be introduced and developed within the factual backgrounds they are set against. And there are costumes to be made, and colossal sets to be built, all researched to look authentic. Writers have to produce dialogue that captures the essence of the period without sounding antiquated, and is easy on the ear of a modern audience. And most difficult of all, the director must have a flair for painting vivid pictures on the huge canvas of a wide screen.

Inevitably, all this leads to tremendous difficulties that often become impossible to overcome. Universal were lucky to have their opus, *Spartacus*, turn out extremely well considering the problems between director Stanley Kubrick and star and producer Kirk Douglas. 20th-Century Fox nearly went broke with *Cleopatra*. Columbia got away with it with *Barabbas*. Paramount preferred to sit back and rest on their laurels after

74

The Ten Commandments. United Artists put into production a massive tale of the Gogol classic, *Taras Bulba,* only to discover by the time of its completion that three-hour pictures were falling by the wayside – so they made drastic cuts, many of which can be clearly seen, reducing it to two hours. Warner Bros had already come unstuck with *Helen Of Troy* in 1955, and preferred to leave the genre alone.

But MGM, dizzy with the sensational success of *Ben-Hur* seemed to suddenly split their product into two areas – modest pot-boilers and super-spectacular blockbusters. *Ben-Hur* encouraged them to join forces with independent producer Samuel Bronston to film *King of Kings,* and to go it alone with their own mammoth effort, choosing a subject that had proved profitable in the past – a remake of *Mutiny On The Bounty.* Originally made in 1935, it told the story of the ruthless Captain Bligh (played by Charles Laughton) whose ship, *The Bounty,* was wrested from him by Fletcher Christian (played heroically by Clark Gable) while on a mission to Tahiti to collect bread-fruit in 1789. Following the mutiny, Bligh returned to England to be absolved, while the mutineers discovered and settled on Pitcairn Island.

For Trevor Howard, recreating the role of Bligh, this should have been the one to really put him on the Hollywood map. Why it didn't remains in part a mystery since he turned in a performance as remarkable as anything else he ever did. The only explanation is that in Hollywood you are only as good as your last film. And the consensus of opinion is that the remake of *Mutiny On The Bounty* was a total disaster.

Few films had been plagued with so much trouble, with the possible exception of *Cleopatra.* At the time when MGM were preparing to remake *Mutiny On The Bounty,* they were also about to embark on the first story-telling feature film in Cinerama, *How The West Was Won.* A leading producer from Universal, Aaron Rosenberg, had just been signed to Metro and, as one of Universal's leading exponents of westerns (having made some of James Stewart's most memorable horse-operas), he had been promised the job of producing *How The West Was Won.* But that task, he discovered, had gone to Bernard Smith. Anxious to placate their gifted newcomer to the studio, Metro generously, or so they thought, gave him

Mutiny On The Bounty. For months the MGM research department had been gathering voluminous data from the Admiralty in London as well as other sources of records of the court martial of the mutineers.

While all this was going on, Rosenberg's job was to find a suitable director, writer and cast, and, despite all the MGM publicity material, this was not a piece of cake. 'In selecting the talent to bring *Mutiny On The Bounty* to screen life,' it blurbed, 'everyone concerned with its production was guided by a single consideration – to find the best people of each department.' Aaron Rosenberg, it continued, 'was considered the perfect choice as producer.' Director Lewis Milestone 'brought to the project an inventive and resourceful talent', while Charles Lederer 'was chosen for the Herculean task of compressing the exciting and involved story of the mutiny into a script'.

The first thing Rosenberg did, even before there was any script written or director chosen, was to try and interest Marlon Brando in the picture. In fact neither Milestone nor Lederer were in on the production at the start.

This suggests that the whole thing was to be more of a package than an exercise in creative film-making. They needed a star name to wrap the whole thing around, and at director John Sturges' suggestion Rosenberg approached Brando with an offer to play either Bligh or Christian. Brando rejected the whole idea, but when he read up on the history of the mutiny he became intrigued by the question of what actually happened afterwards on Pitcairn Island. He wanted to know why, within the space of two years, the mutineers killed each other off.

So he told Rosenberg he might be interested in playing Christian if the film would explore those questions. Rosenberg commissioned Eric Ambler to write the script, but when Brando read it he didn't like Ambler's interpretation of the Pitcairn Island scenes, and he turned it down, saying he would only do it if the script was rewritten.

This time the producer gave the job of fashioning the screenplay to Borden Chase and William Driskill. But, even before there was any kind of a script ready, filming had been set to begin on 15 October 1961 and Carol Reed, whose career had been on the decline, was asked to direct.

He accepted but insisted that Trevor Howard play Captain Bligh. It was one of the best decisions made so far.

Brando, meanwhile, didn't like the new script and had a go at writing his own version, which Rosenberg in turn rejected. 'All right,' said Brando. 'But you're making the biggest mistake of your life. You've made nothing but mistakes since this started. If this is what you want, this is what you're going to get. I'll just do anything I'm told.'

By 15 October, the 125 members of the cast and film crew began filming in and around Tahiti. The *Bounty* had been in construction in a Nova Scotian shipyard, and was still not ready, so Reed filmed as many of the scenes set on the island as was possible, until eventually he ran out of scenes. The ship, which had to travel 7,327 miles, finally turned up in Tahiti on 4 December.

Some 7,000 islanders were recruited to appear in the film. For the scene in which The *Bounty* arrives at Tahiti and is greeted by the inhabitants, 5,000 islanders were called to Matavaii Bay. Over the months they all thoroughly enjoyed being involved in the film, apparently oblivious to all the traumas. An enthusiastic 6,055 turned up and none of them were prepared to cut down the numbers to 5,000, so they were all taken on, and of course, each one had to be paid. The entire cost to MGM for the employment of the Tahitians was $2,000,000. The entire population of Bora Bora, some thousand in all, appeared in the stone-fishing scene. And about three quarters of that island's inhabitants opened their homes to the film crew, and since the Tahitian philosophy is 'to sing, to dance, and to love', that must have kept the men very happy.

But there was little happiness among those in creative control: conflicts had arisen over the concept of the film. MGM had simply wanted a remake, but Reed was more interested in exploring Bligh's motivations, while Brando had his own ideas which changed constantly. What all agreed was that the current script was unsatisfactory, and so Charles Lederer began his version.

At some point during all this Trevor is reported as having objected to attempts to soften Bligh's character, saying, 'I call it wrong to monkey about like that with history – to show a real person like Bligh in a false light.' This may have been in regard to the attempts by Carol Reed to try and make the Bligh of this version far removed from Charles Laughton's legendary, cold-blooded portrayal in the original. Trevor had researched Captain Bligh quite thoroughly and decided that this was a man not so much evil as ruthlessly ambitious. Ultimately, his Bligh has genuine touches of human frailty.

As Patrick Newell noted, 'Charles Laughton's era was one of stage actors doing films and so it was larger than life, and Laughton himself was larger than larger than life. And one of the greatest actors. But Trevor was more clever. He put much more into the role of Captain Bligh. It was subtle, and he was wonderful.'

During the early stages of filming the rains came and for more than a fortnight not a single camera could turn. However, there were plenty of lovely and hospitable Tahitian girls eager to keep the film crew happy, resulting in numerous cases of the 'French Malaise' which were efficiently dealt with using antibiotic injections. One star fell victim, too.

Rosenberg grew increasingly frustrated as Reed, unable to get the changes in the script that he wanted, avoided certain scenes. Brando was playing Christian as a fop and Reed took every opportunity to delay shooting his scenes. Rosenberg, feeling the pressure from the MGM echelons, told Reed to film the script as it was. Reed said he'd had enough and wanted to quit. MGM production chief Sol C. Siegel and Rosenberg decided that if Reed was going to be adamant in demanding changes, he should indeed go. Curiously, Brando was against the idea of replacing Reed, but the decision was made and Reed was fired.

Trevor must have been bitterly disappointed to see Reed go. He and the rest of the British cast had no rapport with Brando who was exercising all the creative control he had been promised, even over their roles, and Reed had battled to turn this into something other than a star vehicle for the moody American star.

It was Charles Lederer who suggested that Lewis Milestone, a tough cookie best remembered for *All Quiet On The Western Front*, direct. Just 10 days after Reed left, Milestone began work. It all went very well for the first two weeks, or so he thought, until he noticed that when he called 'Roll 'em', the cameras failed to turn; Brando was talking to the cameraman, and when he finished he nodded and the camera began turning. Wondering what would happen if he didn't say 'Cut' at the end of the take, Milestone stayed silent and the scene continued until Brando finished his lines and gave the signal for the cameras to stop running.

The day that the scene in which the natives welcome the crew of the *Bounty* to the island was filmed was a particularly hot one. Trevor came onto the set, hot and sticky inside his tight breeches, and all ready to go. Brando was a little way down the beach talking to a number of Tahitian girls. Ridgeway Callow, the assistant director, called, 'Mr Brando, we are ready.' Brando ignored him and carried on talking. Callow called him twice more before Brando strolled back to the set, at which point Trevor, furious and ready to explode, stormed off the set.

'Mr Howard, we're ready,' yelled Callow. But Mr Howard had had enough and made Brando wait until *he* was ready to return.

Ridgeway Callow's job was not the easiest one. As well as having to play the go-between for director and stars, this put-upon unsung hero also had the job of struggling with the names of the Tahitian girls during the daily calls for female extras. Names like Tefaaoro, Ahuroa, Marabayshi, Faatiarau, Manitenaro and Teriitemihau were as common to Tahiti as Jane, Sarah and Linda are to us.

The Tahitian leading lady chosen to portray Miamiti, the girl who captures Christian's heart, was 19-year-old Taritatumi Teriipaia. Unable to cope with the constant call 'We're ready, Taritatumi', Callow was delighted to find her name shortened to Tarita for the sake of screen billing.

The on-screen love affair between Tarita and Brando became an off-screen one that resulted in Tarita giving Brando two children. In general, the Tahitian girls seemed to be falling in love with alarming regularity. One girl who should have had a leading role fell for a French soldier stationed in Tahiti and when he was transferred to Algeria, she went with him. Another girl in the cast fell in love with one of the *Bounty's* Nova Scotian crewmen, and when the film was over she sailed back with him to America.

Despite these romantic interludes bringing some pleasure to the proceedings, Milestone was finding the whole exercise an intolerable nightmare. He said:

> I knew we were going to have a stormy passage right away. I like to get on with things, but Brando likes to discuss every scene, every line for hours. I felt enough time had been wasted, but time didn't seem to mean anything to Brando.
>
> After a lot of bad feeling, the next thing I knew was Rosenberg was on the set every day and Brando was arguing about every scene with him instead of me. When eventually the arguments were over, I'd be told Brando was ready for the cameras. It was a terrible way to make a picture.
>
> Instead of boarding the ship at the dock like everyone else, Brando insisted on a speed boat to take him out to the ship when we were at sea. Three weeks before we were due to leave Tahiti he decided to move from the house he had to an abandoned villa some 30 miles away. It cost us more than £2,000 to make it habitable for him in the week or two he lived in it.

By the time the picture was half finished, Milestone had lost all control. He may have been a tough cookie once upon a time, but he was almost 70 now and the rigours of trying to direct a film, let alone one of epic proportions, in which Brando had more control than he did, was more than the ageing director could, or was prepared to, cope with. He concerned himself more with directing scenes in which Brando didn't appear, and he found Trevor Howard, Richard Harris and the others more than willing to respond to him. But when Brando was on the set he'd do little more than call 'Camera! Action!' and let Brando deal with the scene himself.

One day Rosenberg walked on the set to find Milestone with his feet up, reading a copy of *The Hollywood Reporter* while filming was in progress.

'Aren't you going to watch the scene being shot?' demanded Rosenberg.

'What's the point? When the picture is finished I'll buy a ticket and see the whole bloody mess in a theatre.'

On at least two occasions Milestone stormed off the set and threatened to quit, and, strangely, each time it was Brando who chased after him, imploring him to return and promising to accept his direction. For the rest of that day Brando got on with his job, allowing the director to do his, but the next morning Milestone would find Brando once more arguing over every line, every piece of action and every concept that he didn't agree with.

Brando remained aloof from the rest of the cast and Trevor observed that he seemed to talk only to those who were either younger or shorter than he was. He liked to play practical jokes on them, and one day Trevor watched as Brando tried a ju-jitsu trick on a young Tahitian. 'But the young Tahitian turned the tables on Brando and he sulked for the rest of the day,' said Trevor.

While all this was destructive to the overall production, it should perhaps be said in Brando's favour that he did want to make a picture to be remembered, and he felt that since MGM had virtually hung the film on him from the start he would be the one to take the blame if it failed. But a picture like *Mutiny On The Bounty* could never be a star vehicle; its overall canvas was far too broad and involved far too many characters and too many elements. Even though Brando felt that none of the various drafts of the screenplay matched his own concept and, even more disturbing for him, there was still no satisfactory ending, he should have put his faith in a director who was still perfectly capable of turning out memorable pictures. But with all the conflict centred on Brando, it became impossible for Milestone to achieve anything of his own design.

None of this appealed at all to Trevor. He, Richard Harris and other members of the British contingent drowned their sorrows each evening at the island taverns. Apparently one evening they all returned to their temporary abodes minus Trevor. No one knew where he'd disappeared to. The following morning the actors and crew of the *Bounty* were called on board at 7.30. Trevor was nowhere to be seen. About an hour and a half later a police wagon drew up at the dock. Trevor, escorted by two gendarmes, climbed out the back and staggered up the gangplank, waving goodbye to the policemen. The *Bounty* set sail and, by the time the cameras were ready to roll, Trevor was in make up and wardrobe, ready for his scene which he performed flawlessly.

For much of the time Helen was with Trevor, but when she had to return home, he was left feeling lonely and thoroughly miserable. According to Patrick Newell:

> He said that he'd never before known such misery making a film. He said 'It was purgatory, amigo, purgatory!' He told me that Brando used to make up his lines as he went along and Trevor refused to improvise on the spot. Then Brando took to wearing cotton wool in his ears so that he couldn't hear Trevor's lines. Why'd he do that? I can't explain. Trevor certainly couldn't.
>
> I don't know if Trevor was pulling my leg or not but he said that it got so bad out there on Tahiti that he even gave up drinking for a while because it just wasn't fun any more. Then he had a go at smoking opium. Really, that's what he said. He was taken to some village elder and given a pipe to smoke. He said it was the best fun he had there and ended up dancing all night. But that was typical of him. He had to try everything in life.

Amazingly, Trevor never lost his temper – or at least, he never showed it. Perhaps if he had blown a fuse, Brando might have been shocked enough to give more consideration to his fellow star, but it's unlikely he would have changed his ways altogether for the duration of filming.

It came as a relief to everyone when it was time to return to Hollywood and the MGM Culver City Studios for interiors to be shot. Over the years since the *Mutiny On The Bounty* nightmare, Trevor said very little about his experience of working alongside Marlon Brando. Often he was completely speechless when asked anything of it. But over a drink he told me:

> As an actor he's a great politician, but because of that he is destructive to those he works with. He was constantly demanding rewrites even on the set, so you never knew

where you were at any time. All the constant changing did was to make the next scene you were doing contradict the one you did yesterday, so all that had to be changed. No, I didn't like Brando. I didn't hate him either. I think he is to be pitied because all he does is make enemies for himself. So he never makes friends. He didn't have a friend on Tahiti – except for the girl he played his love scenes with.

I don't honestly know why he agreed to do the film, except that all he wanted was a 15-minute death scene.

Fletcher Christian's death was the last scene to be filmed simply because it was the last to be written. All along Brando had said he would only do the film if they would show what may have possibly happened on Pitcairn Island. The reason why the mutineers killed each other off is still unknown. So back in Culver City Rosenberg and Charles Lederer asked Ben Hecht if he could come up with ideas that would please Brando. Somehow director Billy Wilder got involved and he suggested that Christian should propose that they all return to England to prove their innocence, and that the mutineers burn the ship to prevent this ever happening. Severely injured in the fire, Christian would then die.

Hecht wrote the scene and presented it to Brando who loved it. By now Milestone wanted nothing more to do with it, so Rosenberg persuaded George Seaton to direct the scene. He said he'd do it only if Brando took his direction. Brando agreed and kept his promise. It took seven days to film, and not once did Brando argue.

The finished film cost $18,500,000.

By the time the film was ready for release, the adverse publicity it had widely received had taken its toll and critics had apparently already made up their minds about it, even before seeing it. Their target was Brando and his performance as a fop. And his death scene. But much of the criticism was mere prejudice. It is certainly a discomfort in the initial scenes to see and hear Brando with his odd English accent. But it's a film that really bears viewing again because what Brando actually did, cleverly if not totally successfully, was to present a Fletcher Christian who seems incapable of leading a mutiny.

Because of the film's title, because of its subject, because of the very fact that Christian was the chief mutineer, the mutiny itself when it happens is no surprise. In the 1935 version, it was obvious all the way through that Clark Gable was the kind of man to stand up to the sadistic Charles Laughton, but Brando invented a character who looked like he might blow over in a draught. Only now and then did he give subtle hints with a mere glance or a momentary change in his voice that he was a man who could change. He carried it all the way through to the mutiny, which comes suddenly and unexpectedly; a marvellous scene with more dramatic impact than either the previous version, or the apparently more accurate film *The Bounty* made more recently. From the moment the mutiny occurs, a change comes over Christian and he is no longer a fop but a man of reason, fair play and immeasurable courage.

As for Trevor, he managed, despite all the difficulties encountered, to create a Bligh to be remembered. Of all the marvellous actors who could have given a convincing portrayal of Bligh, Trevor is perhaps the only one who could do that and manage not to be upstaged by Brando at the same time.

By and large the public ignored the critics and on its initial release the film grossed around $9,000,000 domestic. Its foreign revenue would have been about the same, but following the accepted theory that a film must gross about three times the cost of the production to turn a profit, only subsequent re-runs may have ensured that MGM just about broke even.

Because it failed to break even the first time around, since it had cost far more than it should ever have done, it was considered a commercial failure, and, of course, it was most certainly a critical disaster. Both Brando and Trevor were considered as bad as this, their last film, and Brando had to wait nearly 10 years to be forgiven with his Oscar-winning performance in *The Godfather*. But Trevor never recovered, and while he did make the occasional Hollywood-produced film, it was always playing second fiddle to the likes of Cary Grant or Frank Sinatra.

But the whole fiasco didn't leave him particularly bitter,

and he had some fondness for one aspect of *Mutiny On The Bounty* – the ship itself. The *Bounty*, as part of MGM's publicity campaign, made numerous stops around the world, always to be greeted by enthusiastic crowds. When it came to London it sailed down the Thames. A most thrilling sight for the thousands that lined the embankment was Tower Bridge opening its bascules to allow her to pass. At an exclusive vantage point stood the MGM brass and Trevor Howard. One of the publicity officers, Barton Turner, told me that Trevor positively beamed at the sight of the great ship on which he'd spent so much of his time while filming.

Barton Turner turned to him and said, 'She is beautiful, isn't she?'

As proud as a peacock, Trevor replied, 'Of course. She's mine.'

9

A Slip Off The Stool

MUTINY ON THE Bounty failed to gain the laurels it deserved even though members of the American Academy Of Motion Pictures were obviously impressed enough to nominate it for Oscars in a number of categories. But there is the feeling that a certain amount of politics was involved in preventing it from winning any.

The film was nominated for Best Picture and yet not Best Director. With a few exceptions, a Best Picture nomination usually means a Best Director nomination also: since Oscars were first handed out, most movies that actually won the Best Picture award have also won an Oscar for its director. But *Mutiny On The Bounty* had been made under the guidance of three directors even though Lewis Milestone, who was on it far longer than either Carol Reed or George Seaton, received sole screen credit. There was also the controversy surrounding Brando's interference which, in a way made him the fourth director, and it seems very probable that the Academy felt that they could not nominate Milestone for work he was not totally responsible for. Or it was possible that the Academy membership was registering its objection to the way the directors, themselves members, were used and misused.

Lewis Milestone had won his first Oscar at the very first Academy Awards ceremony in 1928 for *Two Arabian Nights*, and his second Oscar for the 1930 classic *All Quiet On The Western Front*. The fact that he wasn't even nominated for *Mutiny On The Bounty* probably didn't bother him as he felt he was hardly responsible for what went on the screen anyway. But his long and distinguished career and, very probably, his self-confidence had been irrevocably damaged: he never completed work on a film again.

So without the possibility of a Best Director award, the film

An early portrait of Trevor Howard before he found film stardom

With Celia Johnson on the set of *Brief Encounter* (Cineguild), the film that set the actor on course for a long and distinguished film career

In *Odette* (Herbert Wilcox), Trevor portrayed real-life war hero Peter
Churchill. Anna Neagle, then the most popular actress in British films,
had the leading role as the heroic resistance fighter, Odette

Trevor Howard always enjoyed travelling to exotic places to drink with good friends. Here, during the filming of *An Outcast of the Islands* (London Films), he samples nothing stronger than the milk from a coconut

Trevor Howard played a South African police commissioner and Elizabeth Allan his wife in *The Heart of the Matter* (British Lion/London Films)

Attending a British film festival with Rosamund John,
a leading lady of British films during the Fifties

There was conflict on and off the screen between Trevor Howard and Marlon Brando in *Mutiny on the Bounty* (MGM/Arcola). In this scene, Captain Bligh (Trevor Howard) is taken prisoner during the mutiny led by Fletcher Christian (Brando)

In their bid to escape from a war-torn Europe in *Von Ryan's Express,* Trevor Howard and Frank Sinatra disguise themselves. Off screen, Trevor found working with Sinatra something of a bumpy ride

During the filming of *The Golden Salamander* (GFD/Pinewood) in North Africa, Trevor samples the local transportation in the form of a camel!

With Yul Brynner between scenes on location in Spain for *The Long Duel* (Rank)

Lord Cardigan, brilliantly portrayed by Trevor Howard, rides back over the battlefield in this scene from *The Charge of the Light Brigade* (United Artists/Woodfall)

One of Trevor Howard's finest roles – as the Irish priest in *Ryan's Daughter* (MGM).
But making the film with David Lean was not a happy experience for the actor

During the Seventies there were many cameo roles, often in spectacular productions
In *Mary Queen of Scots* (Universal), Trevor Howard played William Cecil

One of Trevor Howard's favourite roles was as the Cheyenne chief in *Windwalker* (Pacific International Enterprises). It was a beautiful, compelling film but no major distributor was prepared to find an audience for it

During the Eighties, Trevor Howard sought more challenging roles and won critical acclaim as the eccentric aristocrat in *Sir Henry at Rawlinson End* (Charisma)

could hardly hope to win a Best Picture Oscar. It was also nominated, and rightly so, for Best Photography by Robert Surtees, Best Music by Bronislau Kaper, and Best Song, 'Follow Me', by Kaper and lyricist Paul Francis Webster. And while it's possible to go on about how great an actor Trevor Howard was and how he rarely gave a poor performance, surely his Captain Bligh was deserving of a nomination? Richard Harris also did exceptionally well in what was really a major supporting role and should arguably have been considered for a Best Supporting Actor Oscar. But because neither Trevor nor Harris were particularly kind in their remarks about Brando, there may well have been some bias among their American peers. In fact, the nominations the film did receive were for work produced by eminent Hollywood names, and the denial of recognition to the British contingent would seem to indicate that Trevor and Richard Harris, the two most prominent British actors in the cast, were unlikely to be made welcome in Hollywood again.

In Harris's case he had virtually to beg Warner Bros to let him do his next Hollywood picture, *Camelot*.

Returning to Arkley in England Trevor must have felt his chance of a Hollywood career was over, but when I talked to him he didn't reflect on it as a time of despondency:

> Of course I expected much more from *Mutiny On The Bounty*, especially when I first began work on it and we had Carol Reed directing it. But you count your losses and drown your sorrows and get on with life.
>
> And life was pretty good, I thought. I had Helen and after all, old boy, if I'd lost everything else and never worked again, I still had Helen. But I did have work. I had a play, *Two Stars For Comfort*, to do, and the film scripts were still being sent to me, so I knew I still had a career. And I suppose I was at an age when most of us either fade away or become character actors. But I kept on working and, although a good many of the films I did were not the bloody good films you'd hope they'd be, I did them, by God, and made a good living at it.
>
> It's true I became typecast, playing officers in war

films or police inspectors or intelligence officers and always with a stiff bloody upper lip, but I still got to do what I felt were more worthwhile roles in TV and the odd play or two.

By this time, however, Trevor's enthusiasm was no longer fuelled by an ambition to become a great actor, but rather it seems by the necessity of being a working actor. Acting was a way of making a living. A very good living, and one which allowed him certain privileges. Like travelling. And so, even before the predictable critical and public response to *Mutiny On The Bounty*, he began accepting film roles that, from their often lacklustre screenplays, could offer little more than money and exciting locations.

In fact, immediately after returning home from the nightmare of working with Brando, and prior to the play he was set to do, he and Helen once more packed their cases and took off for another exotic film location, this time in Kenya for *The Lion*.

William Holden was the leading man. He played a lawyer who comes to Africa to visit his ex-wife (Capucine) and discovers that his daughter (Pamela Franklin) has befriended a wild lion. Trevor had little more to do than play the friendly big-game hunter.

For Holden it was a chance to make the one film that reflected his interest in big-game preservation, and it was in Kenya that he founded a game-preservation farm, the Mount Kenya Safari Club. Holden was an American actor Trevor had enjoyed working with on *The Key*, and if Trevor's supporting role and the moderate melodrama itself were hardly enough to excite him, he could at least rely on Holden's enthusiasm to join him occasionally for a drink after a hard day's filming. Holden once said to me of Trevor:

I like him. I like him because he has no pretensions. He was never the great 'I am' and doesn't try proving what a big star he is, which even I could be accused of on occasions. Sure, he enjoyed a drink and when we did *The Key* there was Trevor and Carol Reed and Bernard Lee having a good time, you could say.

When we made *The Lion* in Kenya he brought his wife Helen with him, so there was a lot less of the 'Come and have a drink, old boy'. They're such a devoted couple and he liked to spend time with her. But every now and then we'd get together after filming and toast each other's success.

What struck me about him was that he didn't seem particularly ambitious. He talked about cricket a lot, which didn't really interest me much, but he seemed to have a sense of growing dissatisfaction with acting and told me he wished he'd taken to playing cricket instead. Now, I've no idea what kind of contribution he would have made to cricket, but I do feel his contribution to acting was far more than he seemed to realise. If he'd given it up, I think he would have left a hole.

He also talked about his life in England and about his cottage. He used to say, 'You must come and stay, old boy'. But you also felt that his home life was one far removed from being an actor. He adored his wife Helen and I think he was, when we made *The Lion*, seriously thinking about, not retirement, but accepting the fact that he might eventually lose heart for acting altogether. But I told him he should never give up because he was such a wonderful actor and he would never be out of work. He used to say, 'You got it right, old boy. You got a piece of *Bridge On The River Kwai* so you'll never go broke if you never act again.' But then I never thought I was as good an actor as he is, so I was prepared to go under, though, thank God, I haven't so far. But he can go on for as long as he's got breath.

Part of Trevor's admiration for Holden certainly seems to lie in Holden's wily dealings with major film studios. Said Trevor:

You've got to hand it to Bill Holden. He was the one actor in *The Bridge On The River Kwai* who seemed to figure it was going to be such an enormous hit and, while Jack Hawkins and Alec Guinness accepted a flat fee to do it, Bill insisted on 10 per cent of the profits to be paid yearly, and that, he told me, worked out to about $50,000 a year.

After that he was in such big demand he was getting like 20 per cent of the profits from his films as well as a huge fee up front. When we made *The Lion* he must have been one of the highest paid actors around. But he never let it go to his head. But I do think he drinks too much. Not a good thing for his liver. Happily I've got low blood pressure so I can drink as much as I like, amigo!

Well, that was Trevor's excuse for the amount he drank, and one he apparently stuck to for years.

The Lion's director was Jack Cardiff, Trevor's guiding hand on *Sons And Lovers*. But *The Lion* was not destined to become another commercial and critical success, and Cardiff in time would give up his directorial chair and return to displaying his greater talent as a cinematographer. Out of the handful of films he had directed, Trevor starred in three. Said Jack Cardiff:

I'd always look for a part for Trevor if I directed because he was one actor I could rely on to be on time, remember his lines and give a first-rate performance without me having to explain it all to him. All that stuff about him going off on a binge and raising hell is all nonsense. I never saw it happen anyway.

The only time he missed a few days was when he was involved in a car crash when we were doing *The Lion*. Helen was with him and they were both hurt. I think Helen broke an arm and Trevor was badly cut. It was just an unfortunate accident and he had to be stitched up, but after just a couple of days he was back at work.

All Trevor said about the accident to me was, 'It was one of those things. My main concern was for Helen who was quite badly injured. I thank God it wasn't worse. If I'd lost my Helen . . .'

As soon as he had finished on *The Lion*, Trevor began in *Two Stars For Comfort*. While shooting the interiors of *Mutiny On The Bounty* at the MGM Culver City Studios the previous year,

Trevor had discovered a nearby restaurant, The Retake Room. One evening, taking solace there from the rigours of working with Brando, he had met playwright John Mortimer who sounded him out on the idea of doing a play together. They agreed on *Two Stars For Comfort* over a drink. Almost at the same time he was approached to appear opposite Ingrid Bergman in a BBC–CBS co-production for TV, *Hedda Gabler*.

With two projects he considered worthwhile, some of the old acting zeal became more evident and, hardly drawing breath after finishing filming in Africa, he submerged himself in work. But for once he had taken on more than he could cope with.

Two Stars For Comfort opened in Blackpool and then moved to the Garrick in London in April 1962. While performing by night, he began rehearsing *Hedda Gabler* by day. It was an adaptation of Henrik Ibsen's play, produced by David Susskind, Norman Rutherford and Bergman's husband Lars Schmidt, and directed by Alex Segal. Michael Redgrave and Ralph Richardson were also among the distinguished cast. But, on the whole, this was a star vehicle for Ingrid Bergman and, with her husband as one of the co-producers, he was on hand to offer her advice and even a certain amount of direction. The play was recorded in three days but wasn't aired until a year later when the *Daily Telegraph* said of it, 'Well, if old Ibsen must be bolted through in 75 minutes flat, who better to do it than Ingrid Bergman, Ralph Richardson, Michael Redgrave and Trevor Howard.'

The strain of filming *Mutiny On The Bounty* and *The Lion* on top of each other, and then stepping straight onto the stage as well as doing a TV play took its toll, and Trevor decided to turn to a drink for solace after the recording of *Hedda Gabler*. It was a long, unhurried session that took him way over the legal limit for driving, but he nevertheless decided to drive himself home, and in the early hours of the morning he crashed into some roadworks. The police were immediately on the scene. They had Trevor walking up and down the white line in the road and he complained that they should be looking after him instead of making him take part in what he considered 'this nonsense'. He was subsequently ordered to appear in Court in September.

Meanwhile he continued in *Two Stars For Comfort* and, unlike previous occasions when he had dropped out before the end of long theatrical runs, he stayed the course for its six months' stint.

A month before it closed he made the headlines by appearing in Court on what proved to be his second drunk-driving offence. He had at some time previously been charged and had got off with a warning. A second offence had more serious implications, and he faced the distinct possibility of a prison sentence.

In representing Trevor, Mr Christmas Humphreys QC decided to seek the Court's leniency. He told the Court that his client had been working for 10 months solid on films without a holiday, and then had worked a further month for 16 hours a day doing the play and *Hedda Gabler* prior to the incident. He said that Mr Howard had been drinking 'to give him the energy to carry on a task that was almost more than he could bear'. He assured the Court that Mr Howard was going to take a holiday as soon as his play was over.

There was some light relief as the police described their lack of amusement at Trevor's insistence that they should be taking care of him instead of making him walk up and down white lines. The Court rightly took a dim view of what was a serious offence and Trevor was told, 'You are a man who drinks vast quantities every night. You have so little care for your fellow citizens that you are willing to drive.'

However, the Court decided that to put Trevor in prison would not be in either the public's or his own interests, so he was fined £50, ordered to pay £30 costs and disqualified from driving for eight years.

He had got off lightly and, some might argue, unfairly since far less famous citizens have rarely been that lucky. But he did seem to have learned his lesson, although he didn't have the opportunity to make the same mistake again for the next eight years as he had to be chauffeured everywhere.

It was the kind of incident that only reinforced the Press portrait of Trevor as a hellraiser. But the reality was that while drinking and driving was a foolish error on his part, he never set out to cause, or be the cause of any kind of trouble. As Patrick Newell told me:

He was not the sort of fellow who said 'For art's sake have I broken up the bar.' Not that sort of man at all. Oh, he slipped off the old bar stool occasionally and when going home tripped over the odd stone that he was sure wasn't there when he went out. But he wasn't like some I could mention – never that sort of noisy, knocking it down guy.

He really liked people. When he walked into a bar he knew the name of the barman within five minutes, so he could say 'Ah, Harry, another Worthington.' He knew the name of the man he was talking to, and he knew the name of the waitress who was bringing sandwiches.

He was gregarious but not over the top. He would name four or five people we were working with and I'd think, 'Christ, I've known all these people for weeks and I can't remember their names.' But he would know them all. He didn't sit down and study them. He didn't have a list and think, 'I must know all the names of these people I'm working with.' He'd simply know their names because he'd met them. And in this business you meet thousands of people.

Perhaps that's why he called everyone amigo because he could make friends so easily. Why it was 'amigo' I don't know, but he had a great time calling everyone amigo, like David Niven used to call everyone 'old bean'. It sort of fitted in really with his voice. A most distinguished voice. Beautiful voice. I can hear him now. 'Ah amigo!'

10

On Board With Ol'
Blue Eyes

HAVING SURVIVED THE long run of *Two Stars For Comfort* and
the drunk-driving incident, Trevor took Helen off to a hotel
near Nice in the South of France for a much-needed period of
recuperation. Then, during 1963, he flew to America to star in
The Invincible Mr Disraeli for the Hallmark Hall of Fame TV
series. His co-star was Greer Garson and his director, George
Schaefer. If Trevor knew anything of Schaefer's work he would
have been grateful he was in such capable hands. Schaefer's
work on American TV was prolific to say the least, and his
many productions had earned him a total of eight Emmy
awards. And for his portrayal of Disraeli, Trevor won his own
Emmy.

He accepted his next assignment eagerly as it was to co-star
with Robert Mitchum. They had developed quite a rapport
while filming separate projects in the Mexican jungle in 1956,
and *Man In The Middle* was to be their first of two films
together. It was only the prospect of working with Mitchum
that prompted Trevor to do what was another typecast
cameo. He was bored by the screenplays being sent to him,
although this one, directed by Guy Hamilton who had
directed him previously in *Manuela*, offered some courtroom
intrigue which he and Mitchum had felt could work well.

Mitchum played an American soldier stationed in India at
the end of World War Two who shoots a British sergeant and
stands trial for murder. The crux of the story is whether or not
Mitchum is insane, and it's up to military psychiatrist Trevor
Howard to find out.

As with so many of Trevor's films, his brief appearance was
powerful enough to move the *Evening News* to comment,

'Mitchum is the star but Howard takes command.' And hard-nosed American critic Judith Crist wasn't at all impressed. She wrote, 'For once Mitchum seems to have an excuse for keeping his eyes at half mast.'

Mitchum, of course, is another of the so-called 'hellraisers', but Trevor has always disagreed with that description of his friend. 'Bob Mitchum works diligently when he's needed to, and, well, he has been known to crack open a can of beer afterwards. But at heart he's a quiet, home-loving man. Been married even longer than I have.'

However, while *Man In The Middle* was being filmed in India and in England at Elstree Studios, Mitchum and his wife Dorothy were only just overcoming some marital difficulties after rumours that he was having an affair with Shirley MacLaine. By the time the Mitchum family, including children Chris and Trina, came to England in 1963 for the filming of *Man In The Middle,* some semblance of normality had returned to the marriage. While making the film Mitchum became aware that it was not going to be particularly memorable after all, and, feeling increasingly disenchanted with movies while increasingly happier with his home life, he announced that he was going to retire. Of course, he never did.

Despite the hard-drinking, hard-living image of Mitchum (who a few years back entered the Betty Ford Clinic in Palm Springs to dry out), he does have a softer streak to his nature, and the musician within Trevor was delighted to discover that during breaks in filming Mitchum would chase away the tedium by bursting into song. Consequently their friendship strengthened, and the Mitchums and the Howards would visit each other, either in Arkley or at the house Mitchum had rented five minutes from Elstree Studios. 'You could see that they were great buddies,' Ken Furgeson, editor of *Photoplay* told me.

In all the films Trevor made during the next eight years until his driving suspension was lifted, he was never seen actually driving, and all scenes in which it was essential to see him in a moving car had to be done in a studio mock-up or writers had to find a way for him to be chauffeur-driven. Ken Furgeson 'went down on the set of *Man In The Middle* to

interview Bob Mitchum, and I watched Trevor Howard do a
scene in which he was supposed to get into a jeep and drive
off. He was under suspension from driving and so they filmed
him getting into the car and then cut away so a stand-in could
get in and drive it instead.'

When the film was over Trevor took the opportunity to go
to Lord's to watch England play the West Indies. One day
while watching the match he was approached by playwright
Michael Mayer who had translated Strindberg's *The Father*.
They struck up a friendship, and when producer Casper
Wrede decided to stage Mayer's adaptation of *The Father*,
Mayer suggested he cast Trevor in it. This was to be Trevor's
last major play for some years. It opened in Brighton but was
not very successful and ended on a gloomy note in London at
the Queen's Theatre. Its failure didn't help Trevor's growing
disenchantment with the theatre. He decided to stick to
movies and continued to make down-grade pictures.

By 1964 the James Bond movie cult was in full swing and'
everyone was jumping on the bandwagon, with copy-cat
movies like *Our Man Flint* and *The Silencers*, the latter being the
springboard for a series of Mat Helm adventures starring
Dean Martin. These films were sometimes successful but most
of them were simply short-lived super-spy capers from
America. British director Jack Cardiff came up with the new
slant on the theme of indestructible spy heroes with *The
Liquidator*. This was a spoof that had a reluctant hero, not a
ruthless killer in the 007 mould but a mild-mannered café
owner, played amusingly if not believably by Rod Taylor, who
is unwillingly enlisted by British Intelligence to liquidate
enemy agents. The film even featured an 'M'-type character,
played in the Bond movies by Trevor's drinking partner,
Bernard Lee. In *The Liquidator* the role had to be played with
ruthless authority but with tongue firmly in cheek. Cardiff had
no hesitation in offering the role to Trevor, who carried the
part off superbly.

Unfortunately the rest of the main elements in the film
failed to work and it was an uneven affair. It was
commercially necessary to feature American star names so
that the film appealed to a Stateside audience. In the result,
the cool, American beauty Jill St John struggled with a false

English accent, while Rod Taylor, born in Australia but a star of Hollywood films since 1955, sounded far too American throughout, and had too much of a tough-guy screen image to be believable as a peace-loving wimp.

But the whole thing was enlivened by some home-grown talent that helped to carry the joke off, particularly comedian Eric Sykes as the professional murderer hired by Taylor to do all the liquidating.

Also effective was David Tomlinson, fresh from his success as the harassed father in *Mary Poppins*, playing a cold-blooded double agent in a bowler hat. But their appearances were all too brief, and it was left to Trevor to keep the joke going as the cunning intelligence officer whose itchy neck is more reliable than his own instincts when trouble is afoot. He played the part with all the gruff cynicism he was famous for, believing he knew a killer when he saw one and telling the terrified Rod Taylor, 'You're not fooling me for a minute. You love your work.'

Another clever touch was from composer Lalo Schifrin who came up with a title song that sounded like a genuine James Bond theme. It was all the more effective as it was sung by Shirley Bassey who went on to record more Bond themes than any other artiste.

In the hands of a more inspired director and with a British and less heroic-looking actor than Rod Taylor in the title role – David Niven, for instance – *The Liquidator* could have been a classic.

Legal wrangling over the copyright kept the film shelved and it was not released until 1966.

In 1964 Trevor was delighted when Hollywood gave him another chance and he flew off to the South Seas to play second fiddle to Cary Grant in *Father Goose*. This was one of a number of films made at that time for Universal in which Grant functioned as star and producer, and Trevor was actually Grant's own choice of actor. Although he was Grant's personal choice, Trevor may well have felt some misgivings about embarking on another Hollywood project which was under the influence of its major star. However, Grant proved not only amiable but was prepared, even determined, to shock his fans with a totally new image. He instructed the publicity office to release alarming reports of an 'unkempt, unshaven, grubby-looking' Cary Grant. What audiences saw on the screen was a now totally grey-haired Grant, complete with stubble and minus the usual immaculate suit. Instead he wore the casual attire of a Pacific Islands beachcomber, forced by Australian naval commander Trevor Howard into manning a strategic South Seas watching station during World War Two.

Trevor actually played few scenes with Grant since their communication in the film was over a radio. It was often hilarious. He told me:

> Grant was always there on the set, overseeing the entire operation whether or not he was in the shot. If a line of comedy didn't work he'd immediately call for his writers (of which he had three) to polish it up, and, consequently, I think I played some of my best comedy scenes ever in *Father Goose*.
>
> I was grateful to Cary for that. Of course, it was his film and he came away with the biggest laughs but the comedy worked because he made sure that the dialogue we had together, even if I was basically his straight man, was slick and funny.

The film was a huge success and the screenwriters Peter Stone and Frank Tarloff won an Oscar. Upon acceptance of it Stone said, 'My thanks to Cary Grant, who keeps winning these things for other people.' Trevor might have added his own thanks if he'd had the chance because the film revived some interest in him from the American studios. However, this interest was not sustained – by this time he had become identified with a British military type, for which there was little call in Hollywood.

That image became unshakeable, and very likely by this time he wasn't prepared to bite the hand that fed him, so when MGM offered him a cameo star part in their expensive war picture *Operation Crossbow* in 1965, he took the money and ran right along with it. It wasn't much of a film, or a role for him, but it was typical of a lot of the work he was offered and accepted.

At least the next offering, *Von Ryan's Express,* in this genre gave him a starring role, albeit again opposite another major American star, and it proved to be a far superior picture all round and surely one of the best war films of the Sixties.

Films like *The Bridge On The River Kwai, The Longest Day* and *The Great Escape* had brought the genre of war pictures into the super-production bracket. In fact, after the disastrous effort by Fox to make the ultimate epic, *Cleopatra,* it was *The Longest Day* which saved the studio. Then, when the classic POW picture *The Great Escape,* and the more modestly budgeted but still spectacular *The Train,* both proved so incredibly successful for United Artists, Fox came up with an idea for another large-scale war picture, in part *The Great Escape* and in part *The Train.*

While these attempts at jumping on bandwagons have often fallen flat, *Von Ryan's Express* was a huge success, critically and commercially. And under the direction of Mark Robson it avoided the comic-strip heroics of *The Great Escape* while keeping it on an even *Boys' Own* adventure level without making any attempt at the somewhat flawed stark realism of *The Train.*

Trevor was the suitably gruff and ruthless British Army Major in the Italian POW camp, and Frank Sinatra the American flier who finds himself at loggerheads with the Major. When the Italians change sides, the POWs escape, are recaught and placed on a train which they then commandeer to use in their escape to Switzerland. The film had plenty of nail-biting tension, action, pathos and humour and, unlike most other large-scale war movies of the Sixties, it didn't feature dozens of star names. Most likely Fox had to pay Sinatra a hefty sum and were not prepared to pepper their product with lots of expensive cameos. Indeed, the film didn't need it. But what they did do for a little insurance cover was to feature pop star John Leyton in a supporting role. He had made his film début in *The Great Escape,* gaining it a healthy teenage audience, and, while Leyton never became a major movie star and is now all but forgotten, he did make a number of the best war films of the Sixties.

Just exactly how Trevor and Sinatra got on during the making isn't totally clear. There seem to be some contradicting stories. Trevor himself apparently enjoyed working with Sinatra: he told me, 'I always say that it's a bonus to be billed alongside Frank Sinatra.'

But during filming there was a great deal of typical superstar treatment for Sinatra while, equally typically for a Hollywood production, there seemed little for Trevor. Sinatra is also renowned for not being the most gregarious of people except with his Rat Pack buddies. And his temperament is one that the Press exploit: they overstep the mark and give him cause to explode as furiously as they want him to. As for those who work with him, some he takes to, others he doesn't.

One of the cast, James Brolin, then a bit player before Marcus Welby made him a star on TV, gave me his version of what it was like to work with Sinatra and Trevor:

> Trevor was so good. He was wonderful. He would sneak off every once in a while and take a drink and one drink would just have him ploughed for the day, so he had to have a sort of guard with him. But he was such fun and so damned good. I have such respect for brilliant actors who work with such ease like that.
>
> Sinatra was more difficult. Sinatra was sort of at his prime at that time. He would arrive at these distant locations in Italy in a helicopter, and one day he would say 'Hello Jim, how are you today?' and the next day you could say 'Hi Frank' and he'd walk right by you! You never really knew where he was going to be at. I don't know if chemically he'd change from day to day or if his stars weren't right, or if maybe that was just the game he played. If Brando plays games at least he is consistent about it. You know if you run into Brando he's going to play mental chess with you, but with Sinatra you never knew what the game was.

It would seem that a chameleon character like Sinatra's was unlikely to endear itself to Trevor. John Leyton painted a different picture of Sinatra but conceded that Trevor didn't seem to take to Ol' Blue Eyes. When I talked to him he gave some insight into some of the problems Trevor, and everybody else, had in working with Sinatra:

It wasn't a happy movie and I don't think Trevor got on with Sinatra and I can understand it. Sinatra arrived and left in a helicopter with all his henchmen. It was 'Frank Sinatra and Trevor Howard in . . .' but there was Trevor Howard having to go out on location with me and somebody else, bumping around in this old Citroën, and we'd sit around and grab a butty and a cup of coffee, or in his case probably a glass of beer. We'd be on the set from eight o'clock and by about ten-thirty nobody's shot anything. Then the helicopter arrives. Out steps Frank Sinatra. Everybody's ready for him in front of the cameras. The director calls 'Action! Camera!' and then you hear 'Cut! Print!' and he's back in the helicopter and off home, and we're still standing there. I think Trevor was a bit put out by all this favoured treatment, which is understandable.

When I first got out to Rome I was called the following day to the set where we were filming in a railway siding. I got there and hadn't even met the director Mark Robson until then. And he said, 'Right, we're doing this scene', whatever it was, and it was a scene with Trevor Howard and Frank Sinatra.

Mark Robson said, 'Come over and meet Trevor and Frank,' and I thought 'This is ridiculous' and I pinched myself to see if I'd wake up.

I was taken over and there was Trevor Howard standing to one side and there was Frank Sinatra standing in between two railway carriages, standing on one of the railway lines. And that's where I first met these two screen giants and played my first scene with them both.

Now I'm sure that what Jim told you is absolutely true, and Sinatra could get bad-tempered at times but he never got bad-tempered with me. I found Sinatra charming and got on exceptionally well with him. I'm sure he was pretty nasty to other people in the film, but I can only judge him from my point of view. And from my point of view he was always very nice.

Whether or not Trevor and Sinatra ever got to sit down and have a friendly drink together, I don't know. But apparently for ages after Sinatra boasted that he'd acted opposite 'a guy who makes Dean Martin's drinking look like kid's stuff!'

Although Trevor was nudging 50 and his face was bearing the marks of a life-time of drinking, his active participation in cricket had kept him fit and well enough to do all the running, jumping and fighting the script demanded of him.

On the set Trevor found a lot of the pressure taken off him because the Press were all around Sinatra who'd sit there while the cameras clicked merrily away. Every now and then he'd say, 'Give me 10 minutes would you please fellers,' and they'd go away. On one occasion, according to John Leyton, one of the photographers came back and found himself on the receiving end of Sinatra's fist. If anyone raised any hell on *Von Ryan's Express* it certainly wasn't Trevor.

Interiors were filmed back at the Fox Studios in Hollywood where a very clever set-up was rigged to give the effect of train wheels running along a railway track. As each wheel rolled by, Trevor, Sinatra and Leyton rolled out from under the dummy train in a scene that looked realistic enough to make you think they were all performing very dangerous stunts.

Like Brando in *Mutiny On The Bounty*, Sinatra also wanted his own death scene, although this time it was very quick and extremely heroic. It would have added greater irony if Trevor's Major had been killed instead, since his was the character who had to behave unreasonably at times while Sinatra's role was that of the guy who could do no wrong. An heroic end for Trevor would have been a nice touch.

Trevor thought the film 'was good in its own way', and it proved extremely profitable for Fox. But as strong as Trevor's performance was, it was still little more than a chance to be cast to type in a strong starring role, and Hollywood just didn't have much else to offer him – other than a role opposite the one man he had hoped he would never see again – Marlon Brando.

11

The King and Trev

WHILE IN HOLLYWOOD in 1965 finishing off *Von Ryan's
Express*, Trevor was visited by Aaron Rosenberg, and over a
few drinks they tried not to remember the bad old times. To
his surprise, Trevor learned that, Rosenberg was producing
another picture with Marlon Brando, *Morituri*. After all
Brando had put Rosenberg through, Trevor found this news
hard to swallow.

Brando hadn't been first choice for the film. A number of
other more 'bankable' actors had been approached over the
previous couple of years to do the film but all had turned it
down. Brando heard about it and decided even before seeing a
script that he wanted to play the anti-Nazi German who helps
the British capture a cargo ship. Since playing Fletcher
Christian, Brando had apparently changed his ways and had
gone on to make *The Ugly American* and *Bedtime Story* without
causing problems. He was considered the bad boy of
Hollywood and was intent on proving he wasn't, but he was
having trouble finding the right kind of pictures to brighten
his fading star.

Trevor found all this quite astonishing, but what amazed
him even more was the purpose of Rosenberg's visit. Brando
had personally asked Rosenberg to approach him about
appearing in the film. Understandably, Trevor was very
sceptical.

'He's very keen to work with you again,' Rosenberg assured
him.

But Trevor wasn't keen to work with Brando again.

Rosenberg convinced Trevor that not only was he Brando's
personal choice but that Brando had given assurances that
there would be no repetition of the kind of problems
encountered in Tahiti. Besides, the producer told Trevor, his
role would only take a few days to film.

So Trevor agreed, deciding to let bygones be bygones.

But it was not all calm on the *Morituri* set. Although most of the problems had died down by the time Trevor set foot in the studio, the storm which had hit the production was a clash of egos between the two major stars, Brando and Yul Brynner. The shaven-headed Brynner was, in 1965, one of the most important movie stars, and his electrifying screen presence, magnetism and sexuality were enough to make some women rush out to the hairdressers and have their locks shorn off in imitation of Yul's shiny pate. In fact, on the set of *Morituri* one famed gossip columnist had asked Brynner what he thought of this latest fad among his female fans. He had answered coolly, 'That's their problem.'

The storm had arisen when both stars, neither of whom had apparently read the script before signing to make the film, complained that their respective roles were not as big as the other. The screenwriter Daniel Taradash, with help from director Bernhard Wicki, went back to the typewriter to make the necessary adjustments, but both Brynner and Brando seemed hard to please. By the time Trevor appeared on the scene, with many friendly greetings from Brando, the two main stars had stopped their complaining and knuckled down to an amicable working relationship.

However, the storm had not abated completely. Wicki's style of direction was very mechanical. He spent hours setting up the camera and the lights, using stand-ins instead of the actors, so rehearsal time was sparse, and the actors didn't know what they were going to do until they stepped onto the set for a virtual 'take'. This certainly wasn't to Brando's liking, but Trevor wasn't put out: he was always a more intuitive actor than Brando who used the 'method'. The film also went way over schedule but none of that bothered Trevor who did his few days' work and left.

But then Trevor discovered what he felt he had reason to believe was the real reason why Brando had been so insistent on collaborating with him again. Brando was in the process of suing a newspaper over a report that he was the cause of so many of the problems on *Mutiny On The Bounty,* and in his attempt to win his case it would be helpful if he could prove that Trevor Howard was happy to work with him again. Trevor was furious: had he known of that situation from the beginning he would never have agreed to make *Morituri*.

Finally released as *The Saboteur, Code Name Morituri*, the film was the first of four in which both Trevor and Yul Brynner appeared, although the first three barely brought them into contact with one another. Perhaps this was just as well as Brynner was one of those Hollywood stars Trevor didn't like, but he didn't come to that conclusion until their fourth picture two years later. Only when they shared equal billing in *The Long Duel* did Brynner manage to infuriate Trevor totally.

That same year Trevor temporarily left behind him the typecasting of the big screen to star on the small screen in *Eagle In A Cage* which garnered him an Emmy nomination. His director was once again the award-winning George Schaefer who never did manage to display his remarkable talent with the handful of movies that he made.

Again in 1965 Trevor played opposite Yul Brynner – and a generous helping of other major stars of the Sixties – in a peculiarly conceived and not very effective spy thriller, *The Poppy Is Also A Flower*. It was publicised, rather dishonestly, as a film from the people who made the James Bond movies. It was actually produced by the United Nations as an anti-drugs TV movie. But its director was Terence Young who was fresh from his success as director of the first two James Bond films, *Dr No* and *From Russia With Love*, the latter considered by many to be the best and most realistic of all the 007 movies. It was also from a story by Ian Fleming, so when it was released theatrically in the UK, under the more effective title of *Danger Grows Wild*, the distributors felt justified in their claim.

Trevor Howard and veteran American actor E.G. Marshall played anti-narcotics agents scouring the world in search of drug peddlers, and along the way they meet just about everyone who was then anyone in movies. There was Senta Berger, a stunning Viennese beauty who was considered the new Sophia Loren. And Stephen Boyd at the peak of his tragically short career, with Angie Dickinson playing his wife. Hugh Griffith turned up in his costume from *Ben-Hur* for a reprise of the same role. Rita Hayworth, coming to the end of her career, appeared fleetingly in a scene with Italian heart-throb Marcello Mastroianni. Singer Trini Lopez played himself. Anthony Quayle donned the uniform of an army captain. Omar Sharif, then an exciting newcomer with olive skin and enticing dark eyes, played a doctor. Even Eli Wallach put in a brief appearance.

The film gave Trevor his first opportunity to work with his long-time friend Jack Hawkins, typically typecast as a General. Like his friends, Trevor and Anthony Quayle, Jack Hawkins was consistently donning uniforms throughout the Fifties and Sixties, although he once conceded, 'Although I appeared to have acquired the reputation of being able to make better love to a battleship than to a woman, to be accurate I've played fewer Service types than Trevor Howard.'

Despite their mutual joy at finally getting to make a film together, and to drink together in the South of France where Hawkins' scenes were shot, there was a tinge of sadness about it all. It had become evident during filming that Hawkins' throat, which had received cobalt treatment for cancer, was causing problems again. His voice was faltering during shooting and, tragically, it proved to be the last film in which his voice was heard. The cancer had not been cured and the ensuing operation took away his voice. He did learn to talk again, through a hole in his throat, but even though he continued to make films until he died in 1973, including one more with Trevor, his dialogue was always dubbed by similar sounding actors. Said Trevor:

> I remember one day on the set Jack's voice just sort of gave out, and it distressed him clearly. Later I took him for a drink, and he looked quite ashen, and I said, 'What is it, amigo?' although I knew what was troubling him. He was afraid the cancer had returned but he was trying to be optimistic. He said, 'Nothing to worry about. The doctors gave me the all clear. Besides,' he said, 'I've been to a faith healer and since then I've been fine.' But I think he knew. Just didn't want it to be true, but he was worried and I was worried. But we didn't discuss it. We just got on with things and it was only when he had finished on the film and was set to fly home that I said,

THE KING AND TREV

'Look Jack, if you're not worried then I bloody well am, so see a doctor please, old boy.' I suppose in a way he was far more scared than he would ever let on, but also I think he was incredibly courageous to carry on the way he did through those operations, right up to the time he died. I've had some good friends and Jack was one of them. I was devastated when the end came.

Of all the cameos in *The Poppy Is Also A Flower*, the largest belonged to Yul Brynner who may have felt he was far too important to be wasted in just a few minutes of screen time. Nevertheless, he cut a dashing figure as Colonel Salem, his black shirt and black fur hat standing out stark against the desert background. But over the years his ego had proved too much for many of the actors who worked with him, and he succeeded in making himself extremely unpopular, though not yet with Trevor.

This film was at least something of a departure for Trevor. He once more had a leading role, but one which allowed him a certain amount of action as what amounted to an ageing James Bond. Because all profits from the film were to be donated to charity as part of the UN's fight against drug abuse, Trevor, Marshall and everyone who appeared in it received a 'payment' of £1 each. But they all accepted this willingly, feeling they were fighting for a good cause. Trevor certainly wasn't bothered at doing the film for virtually nothing because, once again, he had the chance to film abroad, and this was a picture that took him to numerous corners of the world.

'Maybe it wasn't the great film we all hoped for,' he told me, 'but I did get a bloody marvellous free holiday out of it – and a pound. That must be the smallest fee any actor ever worked for, amigo.'

As the James Bond movies gradually came to dominate the movie market of the Sixties, so their influence continued on far too many films made at that time. When a German producer, Fred Feldkamp, decided in 1966 to make a film about real-life war-time double agent Eddie Chapman, he wasn't looking so much for an authentic retelling of what was, after all, one of the most fascinating true spy stories of the War, as he was a

James Bond-style thriller. And so, like the United Nations with their film effort, he enlisted Terence Young to helm his picture *Triple Cross*.

Once again Trevor made little more than a cameo, again cast to type as a British Intelligence officer. The role of Eddie Chapman went to Christopher Plummer, and, in the role of a German General, was Yul Brynner. This time Trevor's path didn't cross Brynner's: Brynner was involved in the scenes in which Chapman, having escaped death at the hands of Nazis by agreeing to work for them, undergoes a training programme under the German General's guidance. Trevor only appeared when Chapman comes to England and reports to British Intelligence to tell them of his mission and begin work for the British.

Although Trevor was not really a movie star in the common sense of the word – that is, a personality actor – he was considered a reliable character actor able to play major supporting roles and small cameo roles, but always still typecast. But typecast or not, and however large or small the role, he seemed determined to maintain the screen career he now had, especially as any further offers from Hollywood seemed unlikely.

At the end of 1966, in *The Long Duel*, Trevor was again in uniform, this time circa 1920s as a British police officer in India during the last days of British rule there. He had hopes that this would be a superior film. It was produced and directed by Ken Annakin, an Englishman who had proved his competent craftsmanship as director on a number of Disney's live-action adventures (including *Swiss Family Robinson*) and had become associated with big-budget pictures in *The Longest Day*, *The Battle Of The Bulge* and *Those Magnificent Men In Their Flying Machines*. *The Long Duel* was his own personal production, financed by The Rank Organisation.

It was an ambitious attempt at recreating the days of the British Empire in India but was marred by Annakin's failure to secure a superior screenplay. Ernest Borneman had written the first draft, based on a story by Ranveer Singh. Another writer, Geoffrey Orme, contributed to the script, but it was finally Peter Yeldham who gave Annakin the closest thing to a suitable screenplay.

It told of a police officer, played by Trevor, whose job is to capture the Indian bandit, Sultan, played by Yul Brynner. They develop a strange respect for each other and the officer finds himself in conflict with the authorities and his own conscience. Harry Andrews co-starred as a heartless officer who tries to discredit Trevor, while other roles went to Charlotte Rampling, Andrew Keir and Patrick Newell.

Filming began on location in Spain, then a Mecca for movie epics, and finished with interiors shot at Pinewood Studios in early 1967. By the time they were back in England, Trevor and Brynner were hardly on speaking terms. Had Trevor recognised the genuine arrogance and vanity of Yul Brynner during their earlier but brief associations together, there's no doubt he would never have agreed to work opposite him in a film where they shared equal billing, with roles of equal importance.

Patrick Newell explained:

> Brynner was a very clever actor and I think his king in *The King and I* was definitive. But he was, or so he said, the best at everything.
>
> One day, while we were sitting around having some coffee with a few other actors, he suddenly said, 'Of course, *The Magnificent Seven* would have been nothing without me.' And everyone was muttering names like Charles Bronson, Steve McQueen and James Coburn. I mean, the line-up in that film was terrific, but as far as Yul Brynner was concerned there would have been no film without him.
>
> And then we used to play games with him and we were going to invent a game that didn't exist because whatever you said, Mr Brynner always said, 'Well, as a matter of fact I was world champion pistol shot', or 'I'm the world champion' of whatever it was you mentioned. So we were going to make up a sport to see what he said, and in Spain they play a game called callot. So someone suddenly said, 'There's this really terrific game going on in the square in Granada', and we were just waiting and then Brynner said, 'Of course I'm the South American callot champion.'

I remember Trevor just standing up and looking at him, mouthing a bad word and walking out of the room.

Relations between Trevor and Brynner didn't improve when the unit was shipped back to England for filming at Pinewood Studios. Patrick said:

> At Pinewood one day there was a knock at my dressing room door, and Trevor came in and said, 'Come to my room,' I said, 'Why?' and he said, 'Just come into my room.'
>
> At Pinewood your dressing rooms are on the ground floor in sort of barrack huts. I went into his room and it was pitch dark. He said, 'Have you seen outside?'
>
> And I looked and there was this enormous caravan parked outside, closing off the light through his window. And he said, 'Give you one guess whose that is,' and I said, 'It's Mr Brynner's,' and he said 'Yes, it is.'
>
> There was this veranda on the back of this caravan which Yul Brynner had got from somewhere, and he was sitting on this veranda in his black shirt, black boots and black trousers – he always wore black – and smoking a big cigar, and Trevor said, 'That bastard! We'll see about this.'
>
> So we went out and Trevor said, 'Morning, amigo. Lovely caravan. Quite big.'
>
> Brynner said, 'It's the biggest in the whole world.' And Trevor just turned round and gave it this tremendous kick. There was a loud 'Boing!' and Trevor didn't say any more to him but just went back and called the first assistant director and said, 'I want that monstrosity out of my window.'

There were far more serious incidents involving Yul Brynner, 'to do with embarrassing girls,' said Patrick. One day, for instance, a female journalist came on the set to interview Brynner who, according to Patrick, proceeded to 'make her look pretty stupid in front of everybody on the set.' Patrick thought Trevor was going to hit him, but the first assistant came over and courageously tore a strip off

Brynner. 'But that was the sort of thing that turned Trevor red with fury. Eventually he wouldn't play scenes with Yul Brynner.'

None of this had ever come to light when I previously interviewed Ken Annakin who had diplomatically told me, 'I never had any trouble with Yul Brynner or Trevor Howard. They were both thoroughly professional and pleasant.'

But it would seem that rarely was it directors who fell out with Brynner, while some actors found his ego and vanity far too much to take. There are stories of confrontations between Brynner and Steve McQueen on the set of *The Magnificent Seven* while director J. Lee Thompson, who directed Brynner in *Taras Bulba* and *The Kings Of The Sun*, told me, 'I found Yul Brynner most friendly.'

And no doubt Yul Brynner was trying to be friendly in his own way with his fellow actors, but when there comes a clash of egos, it inevitably erupts into trouble. With him and Trevor it seems to have been not so much a clash of egos but a simple matter of ungentlemanly behaviour – not cricket, as we English might say, or certainly as Trevor would. He didn't seem to harbour much of an actor's ego. When I asked Harry Andrews about Trevor's reputation for being a scene-stealer, he said, 'I hate that word – scene-stealing. Trevor was never the kind of actor to steal a scene. He gave you everything you needed in a scene and never tried to hog it. If he did steal a scene it wasn't because he had set out to do it. He was always generous to other actors.'

Patrick also found him totally unassuming and related an incident to illustrate this. Trevor had called up Patrick's agent while Patrick was in Hollywood and simply said, 'Hello, Trevor here.'

'Trevor who?' asked the mystified agent.

Said Patrick, 'Most other actors would have been outraged at not being recognised immediately, especially by an agent, but Trevor just said, "Oh, sorry old boy, Trevor Howard." He was most unassuming.'

Patrick was a rotund character, famous for the Welsh smocks he always wore and which Trevor took a liking to:

I used to come to the studio in the mornings wearing a Welsh smock because it's very easy just to wear it over your pyjamas! Trevor admired these smocks enormously, so I sent off for one and gave it to him as a present. He was very pleased about that but I don't know if he ever wore it. It was a maroon one. I don't think anyone ever saw him walking down the street in a maroon Welsh smock.

Patrick became one of Trevor's drinking buddies, but while Patrick could certainly enjoy a few drinks, he always seemed quite staggered at Trevor's own capacity for drink:

He used to say he could drink quite a bit because he had very low blood pressure. That was his excuse. I never bothered to look it up or ask anybody if that was true, but he'd say, 'I've got very low blood pressure so it doesn't matter how much I drink.'

He could drink for 24 hours without stopping, but it was not done in a hurry. I remember one day we were at the studio and we obviously weren't going to work. We'd been in make-up and when we weren't called he said, 'Right Dennis, open the bar.'

We sat there and had two or three or four and it got to 11 o'clock and then 12 and we still hadn't been called. It got to about 3 o'clock and we had a few sandwiches and things like that, and we just sat there talking. Then he said, 'Well, we're not going to work today, amigo. I think it's time we had a drink. I'll have a large whisky.'

And we sat there and talked until 12 o'clock at night, and his driver was asleep on the sofa in the hall outside. But Trevor always arrived in the morning as if he'd not had a drink. Amazing.

He never made mistakes. I mean, he made the normal mistakes actors make – fluffed the odd line here and there. But that was rare. He was terribly nice to professional actors because he was a hundred per cent professional. But he hated Americans.

I loved him. Really loved him.

12

At The Crossroads

THE LONG DUEL was certainly a long haul: it took several months to film. Trevor must have wondered if all the effort and tribulation of working with major Hollywood stars in these super-productions were worth it, especially when this film, which came at the tail end of the cycle of epic films, did only moderate business and certainly didn't gain favour with the critics. Its script was far too routine, concentrating on action rather than words, but what it had going for it was a number of well-staged battle scenes, the chemistry of Brynner's screen presence, and Trevor's sheer determination to overcome the pitfalls of the script – which included a trifling love story between him and Charlotte Rampling.

The pleasure in making the film for him was in shooting at Pinewood for several weeks, enabling him to return home to Helen and Arkley every evening. But before long he was back on an aeroplane, heading for Singapore for another Noel Coward story, *Pretty Polly* (retitled *A Matter Of Innocence* for the American market).

Hayley Mills, then 20 and desperately trying to shake off her Disney child-star image, played a prim and proper young miss who goes on a world tour with her vulgar aunt and falls in love with a Eurasian while in Singapore. Trevor portrayed her uncle, a colonial rubber-planter. For once he was able to break his own screen mould, playing a bit of a roué, and he seemed to have a fine old time doing it.

Under Guy Green's direction it was a pleasant, if trite, romantic outing, often at odds with the cynicism of Coward's original story. Coward himself panned both the film and the performances. 'Trevor Howard was horrid,' he said.

After *Pretty Polly* Trevor came to what Harry Andrews described as a 'crossroads' in his life. He had made far too many mundane films. He knew that now, past the age of 50, he faced the distinct possibility of fading from the screen unless something really impressive and important came his way to put him back on top. Or he could just give it all up. Then, in 1967, Tony Richardson sent him the screenplay of *The Charge Of The Light Brigade*, asking him to play Lord Cardigan.

Richardson was, during the Sixties, one of the 'new wave' of British film directors and was heavily influenced by French film-makers, Truffaut in particular. With films like *A Taste Of Honey, The Loneliness Of The Long Distance Runner, Look Back In Anger* and, especially, *Tom Jones*, Richardson was one of the industry's 'hottest properties', to coin a show-biz phrase. During the mid-Sixties he began planning his film of the famous charge, but he didn't want to remake the 1936 classic that had starred Errol Flynn. That had been a romanticised depiction of the tragic charge down the 'valley of death' with no basis of truth in its story. Richardson wanted to make his version an accurate and telling portrait of the men responsible for the tragedy that sent the 'noble six hundred' to destruction at Balaclava during the Crimean War in 1854. His approach was one of black humour that depicted the officers as bumbling and often cruel men.

The screenplay by Charles Wood describes Lord Cardigan, who led the Light Brigade, as having a 'face as crimson as his overalls, his whiskers as gold as his straps'. It was a physical description that Trevor could well fit, and when he read the script he found it far superior to anything he had read in years. His interest captured, he did some research on Cardigan and discovered a depiction of him by historian Cecil Woodham Smith:

> . . . a stern, harsh, suspicious man . . . a throwback, with the military tastes, the courage, the ruthlessness which had earned his ancestors the epithet ferocious . . . wholly absorbed in himself, the rest of the world was an irrelevance . . . an object of pity . . . never let slip an opportunity to be in the fighting . . . a superb and reckless horseman . . . a foxy look . . . the kind of man who talks incessantly of what is on his mind, repeats

hundreds of times and in the same words his own version of events, ignores his adversary's point of view, and is so ultimately able to convince himself that what has happened has not happened, and that black is white.

This description was in total harmony with the screenplay's portrait, and Trevor was hooked.

With his reputation and an outstanding screenplay, Richardson was able to acquire a cast of considerable weight and talent. John Gielgud made what was then a relatively rare screen appearance as Lord Raglan, the supreme commander of British forces who, for 40 years, had been accustomed to executing the Duke of Wellington's plans rather than formulating one. So when war broke out in the Crimea he found himself a general aged 65 who'd never once commanded an army in the field. Harry Andrews played Lord Lucan, commander of the cavalry, whose ideas about leadership and discipline were years out of date, and who concerned himself more with arguing with Cardigan on the battlefield than with trying to win it. David Hemmings, then one of the brightest new talents on the British screen, played Captain Nolan, the young cavalry officer who was devoted to his profession with new ideas about warfare, and whose two books, published in 1852 were eventually to transform the whole concept of the cavalry's role in battle, but only after the tragic charge had occurred.

Vanessa Redgrave then the wife of Tony Richardson, played the fictional Clarissa, introduced to allow a little romantic interlude that thankfully failed to diminish the authenticity of the whole story, Jill Bennett also played a fictional part, as Mrs Duberly, but it was a role cleverly conceived to reveal some of Cardigan's personality. In a delightfully comic seduction scene, she struggles to undo Cardigan's corset after dinner by candlelight, but when she tries to remove her own corset, he tells her to keep it on, saying he prefers his women 'saddled', and proceeds to smack her behind.

Richardson filmed all the Crimean war scenes in Turkey where he discovered two valleys – one going north, the other going south – that were identical to the pictures and lithographs of the actual Crimean setting for the charge. The location was overlooked by a hill from which Lord Raglan had to be able to recognise the valley into which the Light Brigade were supposed to charge, as well as being able to watch the cavalry attack the Russian guns down the other valley.

At the commencement of filming in May 1967, Richardson warned his cast and crew about the dangers of 'epic-itis', and told them that he intended to make a story of human relationships – or rather the lack of them – and he didn't want anyone getting the idea that they were making a colossal extravanganza.

The constituents of the film were, however, certainly colossal. There were 5,000 extras, 3,500 authentic uniforms painfully researched by historical adviser John Mollo, 1,000 horses, and a team of 60 stuntmen under the supervision of stunt co-ordinator Bob Simmons – the man responsible for most of the stunts in the James Bond movies.

As usual, the location filming came first, spanning 12 weeks, and during this time the cast lived in a hotel in Ankara. They drove out every morning at 5:30 to their location, and twice a day they were provided with an extravagant spread of food. The principal players were provided with their own horses so that man and beast could get to know each other. But the Turkish soldiers recruited as extras kept borrowing the horses when the actors weren't around, and Trevor, Sir John, Harry Andrews and David Hemmings found their mounts unco-operative to their individual commands.

Gielgud, who had never learned to ride properly, found it all particularly distressing, especially as he had been thrown during his first riding lesson in Turkey. Consequently Richardson ensured that there were always a couple of people either side of him, holding the horse's reigns in case it decided to bolt.

The days were long and difficult and it wouldn't be unreasonable to assume that, at the end of each day, Trevor made his usual excursion to the nearest bar to knock back a few with his friends. But those who worked with him in the film saw a different Trevor Howard – one for whom this film meant so much that he was determined to stay sober throughout.

Harry Andrews said:

> Trevor realised how important *The Charge Of The Light
> Brigade* was to him because it was a great role, he was
> competing with John Gielgud, he had an important
> director and the film was costing a lot of money. This film
> was his crossroads and he wanted more than anything for
> it to be a success.
>
> Helen came with him to Turkey, which was dead right
> for the film. He usually liked having a drink with the
> boys, but because this was so important to him he kept to
> the hotel and never drank with the boys. Only once,
> when it rained and we couldn't shoot, did he say, 'Come
> on, let's have a drink.'
>
> So he stayed sober throughout and gave what I think is
> one of his very best screen performances. And I loved
> working with him on this film more than the others
> because we had such marvellous scenes together with
> Lucan and Cardigan at odds with each other, and we
> really had some marvellous dialogue.

It was through such scenes as the arguments that
Richardson slowly, but never tediously, led up to the climactic
charge. The poem by Lord Tennyson simply said 'Someone
had blundered', and Richardson wanted to show who it was
and why.

Every scene involving the historical characters displayed,
usually with black humour, the personalities of those
supposedly in control. Lord Raglan is seen as a gentle, almost
senile commander. He sits in his office, worrying about the
war with the Russians, but he isn't sure where the war is. 'I've
got a map of it somewhere,' he says, and when Nolan enters
the office, Raglan asks him, 'Have you got a map?' While in
the Crimea, Raglan wakes up to find the French allies in the
encampment and, thinking for a moment Britain is still at war
with France, panics. General Airey, played by Mark
Dingham, reminds him that they are no longer fighting the
French, but the Russians.

Cardigan is first seen in the film as someone more
concerned with spending some of his vast fortune on dressing

his cavalry in magnificent finery than with turning them into an effective fighting force. To him, being a gentleman was everything, and when Nolan brings a bottle of beer into the officer's hall where champagne is the order of the day, Cardigan accuses him of insulting behaviour. When Nolan protests, Cardigan says, 'I will arrest you. You are arrested. Go to your quarters and be arrested.' It was a true incident that made newspaper headlines and made the army a laughing stock. But Cardigan, unshaken by the public demonstrations against him wherever he went, paid his men a shilling each to line the London streets on Sundays and salute as he passed.

The cruelty of the British Army was also shown in explicit detail. Common soldiers were flogged as punishment and lived in atrocious conditions, while the aristocracy enjoyed extravagant tastes and pastimes. A brilliant touch emphasising this was to interrupt the action occasionally with animated scenes by Richard Williams in the style of newspaper cartoons.

The crucial point of the film was the series of blunders that led to the actual charge. Lord Raglan dictates an ambiguous order, written by General Airey, saying, 'Lord Raglan wishes the cavalry to advance rapidly to the front, follow the enemy and try to prevent the enemy carrying away the guns.' It is Captain Nolan who delivers the message to the strutting Lord Cardigan who impatiently demands, 'What guns?' Pointing down one of the valleys, Nolan says, 'There are your guns.' At which point Cardigan leads the Light Brigade down 'the valley of death' straight into the face of the Russian guns.

Cardigan displays his legendary courage by being the first over the Russian line, but, deciding he should not fight with common soldiers, immediately withdraws while the noble 600 are almost wiped out in the ensuing battle. Riding back over the dead body of Nolan, he asks, 'Has anyone seen my regiment?'

When Raglan blames Cardigan for losing him the Light Brigade, Cardigan first blames the dead Nolan and then Lord Raglan for ordering the charge. He shows the commander the message he wrote and Raglan points out it is not in his handwriting but the handwriting of General Airey, and consequently blames him.

Unfortunately, the big flaw in the film was the charge itself, and critics weren't slow to pick up on this. But, as Harry Andrews explained to me, Richardson found himself with a huge problem in filming the charge: the Turkish army were suddenly called away to war, so instead of the 600 Turkish cavalry originally mustered to portray the Light Brigade at their moment of tragic glory, Richardson had to film the charge with his 60 stuntmen. Trying to make these look like 600 meant that the camera had to be kept in close to the action, so there are no sweeping long shots of the cavalry as there were in the 1936 version. Consequently, the action was confusing and brief, and was hardly the climax Richardson must have envisaged.

Richardson also filmed the clash between French and Russian cavalry that immediately followed the charge, and which ultimately lost the Russians the battle. There are stills of this from the film, but with only 60 stuntmen to portray both French and Russian cavalry, Richardson decided to delete the sequence. The result was an anticlimactic and ultimately disappointing film. Had he been able to shoot the charge and the battle with the Turkish army, as he did the thundering battles that precede the charge, he would have turned out an undisputed masterpiece.

However, it is a film that most of the actors involved in feel justifiably proud of. Harry Andrews spoke of it with some pride and Trevor told me back in 1979, 'I was disappointed that *The Charge Of The Light Brigade* was not better received. It was not without its faults but I always felt that it had some marvellous moments. Turkey wasn't the easiest place to film and the Turks didn't really seem to like us too much and made life difficult for everyone.'

When filming was complete Trevor paid a visit to Cardigan's descendants in the family mansion at Deene Park. He was most cordially greeted, and during his tour of the property he saw the stuffed head of Cardigan's chestnut, Ronald, the very horse Cardigan rode through the Russian cannons at Balaclava.

John Gielgud, who had worked with Richardson previously

in *The Loved One*, thought his role was 'most amusingly written', and in his autobiography the film is one of the very few of all the pictures he has made that he gives any space to. But one of his regrets, as he told me, was never really getting to know Trevor Howard.

I never knew Trevor at all intimately, although I was in several films with him in which we both appeared; but I never had a single scene with him.

He seemed to me very much of a loner. He did once admit to me, when we were in Turkey making *The Charge Of The Light Brigade*, that he had very few interests or hobbies, although he was incredibly keen on cricket and I think he liked jazz. But he envied his wife's talent for company and her enthusiasm for the opera.

He was always immensely generous to me, and watching him work on film locations, he was impeccably amiable and efficient with beautiful manners and unbounded personal charm.

I am sad to think that I never knew him better, but he never suggested our meeting, apart from work, and I fancy he had no taste for parties or small talk.

While on location in Turkey Charles Wood found the personae of Gielgud and Trevor inspiration for a play which he duly wrote. It was called *Veterans* and was concerned with the private lives of actors and the antics they got up to while filming on location. The play opened in Edinburgh in 1972 and starred John Gielgud as Sir Geoffrey Kendall and John Mills as Laurence d'Orsay. But Gielgud knew very well that he was playing himself, and Mills knew he was playing Trevor Howard, and it was not unknown to a certain number of people that the play was about the off-set goings-on during the filming of *The Charge Of The Light Brigade*. *Veterans* became something of a cult play among actors who flocked to see it and loved every in-joke that generally went way over the heads of others in the audience. Trevor thought it an immensely enjoyable joke just to see himself portrayed by his old friend Johnny Mills.

Back in 1967 during the filming of *The Charge Of The Light Brigade*, John Gielgud was probably never aware just how important it was to Trevor to be acting opposite him, knowing that he was one actor who could, for once, steal all the thunder. Sir John had said that they never appeared in a single scene, probably meaning there were never any moments on film that were just between the two of them. But they did in fact appear together in numerous scenes although there was never the same kind of interaction between them as there was between Trevor and Harry Andrews or David Hemmings.

Trevor was in awe of Gielgud and had anticipated the kind of competition he rarely faced from many of his previous co-stars. Not that he had been out to prove he was any better than Gielgud. He simply knew that with so many disappointing films behind him, this was perhaps his last chance to prove himself. Trevor underestimated himself. It was an insecurity that may have been helped had he been aware just how much Gielgud had admired him in *The Cherry Orchard* and *The Taming Of The Shrew*.

As it was, *The Charge Of The Light Brigade* belonged to all the cast. For Trevor it was most certainly a crossroads where he could either sink or swim at the age of 51. In the event it was a turning point for him because he not only rediscovered the enjoyment and satisfaction of acting, but he was once again considered an important actor. Although, following the film, he still appeared in the all-too-occasional poor film, he suddenly found himself in demand for both large and small roles in just about every prestigious production the British film industry attempted. In fact, Trevor became something of an institution in British films, and not even the disasters he appeared in could do anything to keep him out of work for the rest of his life.

Released in 1968, *The Charge Of The Light Brigade* met with a mixed reception from the critics, but United Artists packaged it with all the pomp and ceremony it deserved. Launched with a glittering première at the Odeon Leicester Square, attended by Trevor and Helen, Tony Richardson and other members of the cast, the film went on to become a box office success. Certainly ahead of its time, over the years it has grown in the

13

Eternity In County Kerry

As Trevor said, after making a long, hard film he liked to have a drink, and that's what he did after the final wrap on *The Charge Of The Light Brigade*. For him drinking was a leisurely pursuit that, like cricket, was best appreciated away from his domestic life in the company of friends. And it was a pleasure not to be hurried.

'He did go out a lot,' Patrick Newell said. 'He went out for three days, never for an hour and a quarter. Some years ago I said to him, "I live on Mikolos now." He said, "I've been there. I went to Fulham Road years ago with a friend of mine and we ended up on Mikolos for 10 days." He was inclined to do things like that a long time ago.'

A good many women may well complain about their husbands going off even just for a couple of hours to the pub, but Helen never did. No matter how long he disappeared for, whether it was an hour in the local pub, a day off in Fulham Road or 10 days on some exotic Greek island, she accepted it was part of his lifestyle and never interfered.

'He usually preferred the company of men, staying up drinking and talking of cricket,' she said. 'But I always knew he would come home to me.'

He told me, 'I suppose the one part of my life that I never share with Helen is when I go out for a drink with friends. Oh, Helen and I like to begin the day with a Buck's Fizz and have a sherry later, but I have always loved being with good friends and talking for an hour or so over a few drinks.'

Trevor also loved film festivals and in 1968 he was on his way to such an event in Brazil when he ran into James Fox, then a bright young star in the throes of discovering some of the pitfalls of stardom. He was in a terrible state. A regular user of drugs and a frightened, exhausted young man, he had just walked off the set of *Isadora*, which he'd very nearly finished filming with Vanessa Redgrave. Discovering Trevor was on his way to Brazil for a film festival as well as for a spot of cricket, he decided he'd go with him. So Trevor suddenly had himself an unexpected travelling companion, which suited him fine as he was just as impulsive as Fox was. After spending about a week together, James suddenly decided to go off up the Amazon, inviting Trevor to share in his Amazon adventure.

Trevor was tempted, but he had a film festival to attend and work had to come first. So he stayed behind leaving James Fox to go off and discover the Amazon, himself and, shortly after that, God. Ultimately Fox's new life of religious fervour meant temporary retirement from the screen.

As John Gielgud had observed, outside of cricket and jazz Trevor had few interests to occupy his time, so if there was no immediate work to concentrate on, and cricket was out of season, naturally socialising with a few friends over a pint in whatever country he happened to be in – or turned up in – was going to take up a fair bit of his time. But while he may have occasionally 'been ploughed' – as James Brolin put it – on frustratingly difficult locations, he did refrain from popping off on a sudden whim to exotic Greek Islands or up the Amazon when a film contract had been signed. He always put his work before booze.

And really, he couldn't afford not to, especially now he was in demand for important film projects, such as *The Battle Of Britain* in which he appeared with dozens of other major British stars. It was the kind of thing he could do standing on his head by now, playing Air Vice-Marshal Sir Keith Park, Commander of No. 11 Group at Uxbridge, Middlesex.

The film was an ambitious attempt to portray the 16 weeks during 1940 when the RAF, the legendary 'Few', fought Hitler's massive airborne onslaught for the supremacy of the skies above Britain. Producers Harry Saltzman and S. Benjamin Fisz began preparations to make the film in 1965. Three years later, under the direction of Guy Hamilton, who had directed Trevor in *Manuela* and had also been assistant director on *The Third Man, The Battle Of Britain* began filming.

It boasted some of the most spectacular flying sequences of any war film, and an impressive line-up of stars, many of whom were Trevor's personal friends, including Michael Caine, Harry Andrews, Kenneth More, Laurence Olivier, Christopher Plummer, Michael Redgrave, Susannah York, Robert Shaw, Curt Jurgens and Ralph Richardson. Most of these were seen only fleetingly as the makers attempted to cover every aspect of the operation and introduce a huge variety of mainly factual characters. Although some felt that a running time of 131 minutes was too long, it was really too little time to introduce and develop so many key characters within the confines of a complex story. So, immediately recognisable film stars, almost all of them typecast, filled the roles, very few of whom did little more than contribute chemically rather than creatively. But somehow it was all very confusing as the audience was switched from one location to another in quick succession, and the film became something of a game of 'spot the stars.'

Most of Trevor's scenes were filmed in an authentically recreated RAF Plot Room from where Air Vice-Marshal Sir Keith Park could oversee the defence of Britain's skies. His was a typical piece of typecasting: the audience knew immediately they saw Trevor that he was someone who was going to keep a stiff upper lip and make authoritative decisions.

But *The Battle Of Britain* had too much of everything – stars, battles, money – everything except for a cohesive screenplay and an inspired director. It was baffling and unmemorable.

However, for Trevor the brief experience of acting opposite Laurence Olivier made the film memorable. 'There's a man you admire all your life,' he said, 'hope to one day get to make a film with, and you do only two small scenes with him shot in about two or three days. But it was worth it, old son. And I've known Larry a long time.'

Half the cast never got to see the other half as they all worked on different days in different scenes, often with different units. So old pals like Kenneth More and Harry Andrews weren't necessarily around for Trevor to have a drink with at the end of the day.

All in all it was a noble and expensive effort, costing £5 million, and despite its hulking great flaws it nevertheless was an important film which was well received by the patriotic British public.

As Trevor's participation in *The Battle Of Britain* was brief, he had time to watch some cricket during the summer of 1968, momentarily wishing, as he did from time to time, that he'd taken up cricket professionally instead of acting. As Helen has said, 'I think he would have given up acting if he could have opened the batting for England.'

His next film also kept him at home in England, playing Susan George's grandfather in Richard Donner's *Twinky*. It was a British-Italian co-production in which Susan George as a 16-year-old schoolgirl falls for a 38-year-old American writer of pornographic books, played by Charles Bronson. It was a typical so-called 'Swinging Sixties' sex comedy that didn't amount to much, despite a strong cast (including Jack Hawkins in a small role). But whether or not Trevor knew it at the time, it wasn't such a bad film to be in: Charles Bronson had just become a major star in Europe and any Bronson picture at that time was a guaranteed success on the Continent and in Japan. These two markets combined were as important as America.

Bronson has always been publicity shy and, even before becoming a major star, something of a recluse. Trevor said of him:

> I found Charlie Bronson to be something of a loner. You couldn't dislike the man but you couldn't get to know him either. I only ever saw him when we were filming but away from the set he was always very private and didn't really seem to like to mix. I've not seen all those violent films he's made but he certainly seemed from what I could tell a man who, like me, really enjoyed his family life and he was never pretentious or egotistical. I've not met him since so I don't know if he's changed. We don't tend to make the same kind of films, old boy. *Death Wish* and all that are not my cup of tea.

In 1969 Trevor received something of a radical offer from David Lean – to play a grizzled old Irish priest in *Ryan's Daughter*. This appealed greatly to Trevor who'd never played a priest before. Lean was casting him totally against type, and Trevor loved the prospect. In fact, Lean was casting just about everyone in the film against type. Robert Mitchum was to play an ordinary Irish teacher. John Mills was playing the village idiot. American actor Christopher Jones, then famous as TV's *Jesse James*, was to be an English soldier. Sarah Miles (the wife of Robert Bolt who wrote the screenplay) was the Irish lass of the title.

This was an offer Trevor just couldn't turn down. He hadn't worked for Lean in years, and during that time Lean had become one of the world's foremost directors with his enormous successes, *The Bridge On The River Kwai*, *Lawrence Of Arabia* and *Doctor Zhivago*. The opportunity to work with Lean again was too tempting. Also, it would mean working with his friends Johnny Mills and Robert Mitchum. But more than anything else, it was a role that offered the best acting challenge, with the exception of Lord Cardigan, he'd had in years.

In March 1969 he went to southern Ireland with the rest of the cast to begin filming. They were based at the small fishing village of Dingle in County Kerry on the west coast. It would be close to a year before the film was in the can, and Trevor came to hate the whole expensive enterprise. It was really just a simple love story set in Ireland during World War One, with a touch of *Brief Encounter* about it: Rosie (Sarah Miles) falls for a teacher (Robert Mitchum); they get married; then along comes a shell-shocked soldier (Christopher Jones) with whom Rosie has a passionate affair.

But despite the simplicity of the story line it was filmed by Lean with all the meticulous care and lavish attention of his previous block-busters. He would shoot a scene, study the rushes and then go back to shoot it again, so that progress was very slow. One day he made Mitchum and Sarah Miles sit for six hours in the middle of a field, waiting for sea-gulls to give him the exact shot he wanted. Such attention to every single detail wore down most of the cast long before filming was complete.

At the beginning of the 10 months' schedule everyone was in high spirits, and great fun was had at the boarding house that Mitchum had taken over for the duration. According to Sarah Miles, the entire company stayed there, and when shooting ran late into the evening after restaurants were closed, Mitchum would cook supper for everyone. This was a tremendous boost to Trevor's morale as Helen had had to remain behind in England to do a play. Trevor knew he could count on Bob Mitchum for some fun, and he was greatly amused when tourists, ringing the boarding house to enquire about lodgings, were told by Mitchum in a soft Irish accent, 'Oh, you wouldn't be liking it here any more. Americans are running it now. Nudists, you know.' Some of Trevor's boredom and loneliness was also relieved by joining Mitchum and other revellers in a daily outing to a local pub run by a cousin of Gregory Peck's.

After the first 10 days everyone knew they were going to be in for a long haul: Lean was already a whole week behind schedule. There were numerous hold-ups because of accidents. Christopher Jones, thought by some to be the new James Dean, very nearly went the same way as Dean when he demolished his brand new Ferrari on a narrow, winding road. His survival from the pile-up was little short of miraculous. Trevor ended up in hospital when he fell from a horse, damaging five ribs and his collarbone. But such incidents couldn't compare to the one that very nearly lost Trevor and John Mills their lives only two weeks into the schedule.

There was a scene in which Trevor and John Mills had to come in to shore in a curragh (a small rowing-boat used by Irish fishermen), riding on one of the high waves. It was shot in Coumeenoole Cove where off-shore currents flowed swiftly and dangerously between the mainland and the great Blasket Islands. John Mills spent the morning, which began clear enough, practising alone in the curragh with successful results. The wind then began to rise and storm clouds gathered with surprising and alarming ferocity. However, Lean, satisfied with the way Mills' dummy runs looked through the camera, said, 'Right, we're ready to go. Where's Trevor?'

Trevor hadn't been called. 'Go and dig him out. And hurry,' Lean told an assistant director. A short while later Trevor strode down to the cove in his heavy cassock and huge boots. 'When I arrived on the set the bloody waves were getting frighteningly high and the wind had become a gale,' said Trevor. 'I didn't like the look of it, but one doesn't argue with David Lean. He said, "Get in the bloody boat," so I got in the bloody boat.'

The curragh, with Trevor and Mills in it, was hauled out beyond the breaking waves by six frogmen. Lean waved a flag to signal 'Action'. Mills began rowing ahead of a wave coming swiftly up behind them. It caught the boat perfectly, carrying it along like a surfboard. 'It all went well until the wind suddenly changed and a bloody great wave hit us from the side,' said Trevor. 'I was hanging onto the boat for dear life and Johnny was rowing like mad when we were just tossed into the air like a ruddy great pancake.'

As the boat came down it hit Mills on the back of the head, knocking him unconscious. Trevor floundered, dragged down by his heavy cassock and boots. The frogmen quickly swam towards them, first grabbing Trevor who may well have been at risk of drowning. For John Mills it would have been certain death if they hadn't been quick enough. He was being dragged, unconscious, out to sea by a strong current. The frogmen brought the two half-drowned actors ashore.

'It's funny because at the time you don't think to stop and say "Thanks for saving my life", but Johnny and I owe our lives to those frogmen,' Trevor said. 'I've never felt so grateful in my life.'

With the bulk of filming still to go, Trevor had little to look forward to as one long day merged endlessly with another. He had rarely felt so lonely, despite the presence of good friends. And when Helen did find time to visit him, she also survived an horrific accident: she fell over a cliff and ended up in hospital with a damaged back. But almost from the first week Trevor was so unhappy he didn't even bother to drink. Often he just sloped off on his own for long lonely rambles. With a shooting schedule looking like an eternity, all he wanted was to just get it over with, as did most of the actors. But nothing could hurry Lean, not even MGM whose money he was spending extravagantly. The studio needed this film to be a success and they were gambling on Lean's recent track record.

Things weren't particularly helped by what appeared to be Mitchum's typical casual attitude to acting. He liked to make people believe he didn't give a damn and, occasionally, would purposely wind Lean up by suddenly and surprisingly delivering the goods in one take. Lean would then give Mitchum overwhelming praise to which the latter responded, 'I wasn't too Jewish, was I?'

While Trevor was more amused by these antics than Lean ever was, he didn't play such games. All he wanted was to get on with things. He hated the waiting around while Lean took his time for just the right moment to shoot. Trevor told me:

> If the clouds weren't right he would wait until they were. Mind you, what he did capture on the screen looked beautiful. David has a talent for that and I can't criticise him nor would I, because not only is he a good friend but a bloody marvellous director. But I do think he was trying to turn out something that just wasn't there to start with. He could do it with *Lawrence Of Arabia* and *Zhivago*, but those were films that demanded a sort of sweeping spectacle, don't you think? *Ryan's Daughter* wasn't.

Towards the end of filming Lean took his entire unit off to South Africa for several weeks to film. He felt that the beaches there were far more photogenic than the ones at his disposal in Ireland.

Eventually, at long last, to the relief of the cast, filming was all over. While David Lean set about the enormous task of supervising the editing and scoring of *Ryan's Daughter*, Trevor and Helen retreated to Yugoslavia for a mid-summer holiday. At Dubrovnik they met up with Rex Harrison and his new lady Elizabeth Harris (former wife of Richard Harris). Rex and Elizabeth had sailed down from Italy on a chartered yacht, and Rex suggested the Howards join them for the rest of the cruise. The invitation was accepted by Trevor and Helen without argument. They sailed on to Corfu and the Greek islands. By day they visited the ancient ruins and by night they drank the local wine. Trevor and Rex reminisced about *French Without Tears*, swapped stories and anecdotes and had a thoroughly good time until the holiday came to an end in Athens.

Ryan's Daughter was premièred in December 1970. Lean had fashioned the film into a three-and-a-half-hour extravaganza which the critics did not take readily to their hearts. Neither did the public. The very simple story had become a sprawling epic that some felt was an endurance test.

Trevor was as bored by the finished film as he was making it. His observation was, 'Three hours is a bit long for a trifling little love story.' And noted London-based film critic Alexander Walker wrote, 'Instead of looking like the money it cost to make, the film feels like the time it took to shoot.'

But the film was not all bad: at times it is quite compelling and ultimately moving, and never less than beautiful to look at. Despite being shot in 70mm with stereophonic sound, it actually stands up much better on television where the leisurely pace is much easier to take in the comfort of an armchair than in a cinema seat.

Almost everyone in the cast received good personal notices, and John Mills won an Oscar, as did Freddie Young for his breathtaking photography. Sarah Miles received an Oscar nomination; Robert Mitchum felt he was for once deserving of a nomination, and was disappointed not to get one.

Lean's own personal favourite performance was Trevor's. It was as far removed from the typecast image as anything he had ever done. His hair was cropped and bleached, and his face covered in a white fuzz. The accent was spot on, and he strode about in great clumping boots putting the fear of God into the villagers, but always with an undercurrent of devotion and compassion for his flock.

'It was no great trick,' he told me. 'The character was there in the script. I may have discovered something about the man that priest was when I put on that damned great cassock, but then the rest comes from inside. Acting is all about believing in who you are supposed to be playing, because if you don't, the people who pay their money to come and see you won't.'

14
Running With The Bulls

WHEN TREVOR RETURNED from his Greek Odyssey with Rex Harrison, he didn't have long to sit around idle. He soon left for Sweden and Denmark to co-star with Max von Sydow and Liv Ullman in Laslo Benedek's interesting, but ultimately ponderous, story of criminal insanity, *The Night Visitor*. 'The most intriguing thing about making that film,' said Trevor, 'was that Laslo Benedek had studied to be a psychiatrist in Vienna before he directed films. So he knew a bit about the subject.'

Later in 1970 he played a foreign office diplomat in *Catch Me A Spy*, a co-production between Ludgate Films of London, Capitole Films of Paris and Bryna, the company owned by Kirk Douglas who was also the star of the film. It was a cat-and-mouse spy caper that was never widely seen outside Europe.

Then Trevor left for Italy, no doubt seduced in part by the free travel, but also at the prospect of working with one of the great Italian directors, Luchino Visconti. In Visconti's lavish 246-minute account of the 19th-century mad King of Bavaria, *Ludwig*, Trevor was on screen for only 10 minutes. It was a prestigious film, if slow and overlong.

Back in England he was among the considerable British talent in *Mary Queen Of Scots*, made during 1971. He had the important role of William Cecil, adviser to Queen Elizabeth I, played by Glenda Jackson. Vanessa Redgrave had the title role, and other members of the cast included Patrick McGoohan, Timothy Dalton, Nigel Davenport and Ian Holm. It was filmed on location in England and at Shepperton Studios, where some magnificent Elizabethan interior sets were constructed. The film was produced by Hollywood veteran Hal Wallis whose previous excursions into

British history began with *Becket* and continued with *Ann of The Thousand Days*. But *Mary Queen Of Scots* proved inferior to these: the screenplay was profoundly silly and the direction by Charles Jarrott never much more than routine. It nevertheless reached a wide audience.

In 1972 Trevor co-starred with Sean Connery in *The Offense*, an intense drama about a tough police inspector, played by Connery, who beats a suspected child molester to death. It was directed by Sidney Lumet, the American director who had worked successfully on both sides of the Atlantic, and had also directed Connery previously in *The Hill* and *The Anderson Tapes*. *The Offense* offered Trevor, as another Scotland Yard type, something more than the stereotyped stiff-upper-lip persona so familiar to him. He counted it among his more worthwhile films made during that period.

With so much work to do, it might seem a wonder that he ever had time for any home life, but as he told me:

> I was making films that usually required me for about a week, but many of them were made at Shepperton or Pinewood or on location in England, so, you see, old boy, I probably spent more time at home than anyone else making films.
>
> It allowed me to be with the one person I really only ever wanted to be with – Helen. And we have our lovely house where we've lived for – what? Nearly 30 years I suppose. It's not the sort of place to come to if you want a rollicking good time, contrary to what you may have heard. I like a quiet life. It's the only way a man can keep his sanity in this business. We don't throw big noisy parties. Of course we have friends for dinner, but they are very civilised affairs. Mostly I like to sit back and read the newspaper, listen to some music and watch cricket on the telly. Well, I try not to watch too much cricket, because for one thing I'd rather go to Lord's and watch it, and for another thing Helen walks out when cricket comes on the box. She has her own interests to keep her busy, but what we have in common is a love of friends and a little company. Otherwise we keep a low profile. I'm really just an ordinary chap, you see.

And then I suppose I wasn't really interested in
making a lot of pictures in which I was going to have to
carry all the weight, so although some have said. 'How
can you just go from one small role to another?' I was
having a marvellous time doing the work I was offered
and getting paid. And still am. I'm not exactly crying all
the way to the bank, amigo.

From what Patrick Newell said, it sounded as though
Trevor didn't actually go to the bank very much, anyway. Not
that he didn't have anything to put in it. But as Patrick said:

Money didn't come into his world at all. There's a story
about a drawer in his study that was always full of
cheques. He'd put these cheques away and forget about
them. Thousands of pounds went straight into the drawer
whereas I'm straight down the bank the day a cheque
arrives.
But when you're in his position, a motor car picks you
up, takes you to work, you're fed and you go home and
the wife says 'I've got steak and kidney pudding for you',
and I suppose you don't stop to worry about getting your
next cheque in a hurry.

The film offers kept on coming and Trevor kept on
accepting them, not always for the good. In 1972 he made
what he referred to as 'that bloody awful *Pope Joan*'. It was
based on the legend of a 9th-century woman, played in the
film by Liv Ullman, who disguises herself as a monk and
eventually becomes Pope. The film was directed by Michael
Anderson who had much better luck with his other 'papal'
picture, the much underrated *The Shoes Of The Fisherman*.
Incredibly, *Pope Joan* features among its star-studded cast
names like Maximilian Schell, Franco Nero, Keir Dullea and
Olivia de Havilland. In between moments of piousness, it
featured nudity and brutality, and ended up looking
somewhat like an exploitation film. 'What a bloody stupid
idea it was,' said Trevor, 'trying to make audiences believe a
woman could be the Pope. God knows why I got involved.
Must have forgot to read the script!'

He obviously took a closer look at the script of *A Doll's House*, sent by director Joseph Losey, the American expatriate who had been blacklisted by Hollywood in the Fifties and came to England to make a number of superior films including *The Servant*, *King And Country* and *The Go-Between*. However, his work was inconsistent, and pictures like *Boom!* and *The Assassination Of Trotsky* failed to display his considerable talent. But Trevor felt that Losey was someone who could translate Ibsen's play into valid screen terms.

Trevor arrived in Norway in November 1972 with other cast members David Warner and Edward Fox, and there they met the star of the film, Jane Fonda. She was then at her radical peak, and she was intent on being characteristically radical with Ibsen. After a week or so of filming, she and Losey were at loggerheads over the concept of the film. 'That was a nightmare,' said Trevor. 'It was winter and very cold and all I wanted to do was play the part of Dr Rank the best I could and hope to God to please the director. That's what actors are paid to do. But every scene had to be fought out between Losey and Fonda.'

Losey wanted to remain faithful to Ibsen's concept of 19th-century liberated womanhood, but Jane Fonda felt that, in the age of total Women's Lib, her role of Norah should be more defiant. She even brought ammunition in the form of her own scriptwriter, Nancy Dowd. Fonda and Dowd would have their own script conferences and then Fonda would inject her ideas and dialogue into whatever scene they were shooting. Hostility of the crew towards Fonda became quite open. Their allegiance, with the apparent exception of a couple of key technicians, was to Losey, and each day inscriptions about Women's Lib appeared on the camera.

Trevor steered clear of all the trouble. According to Jane Fonda, 'Most of the men were drunk all the time. And of course they interpreted anything we did as simply wanting more lines to say.'

The result was a film that, never destined to be commercial, failed to be an 'art movie'. In its favour, however, another version of the same play had been directed that same year by Patrick Garland, a much stagier production, and most critics comparing the two versions agreed that Losey's version was superior.

In 1972 Trevor made a brief return to the stage appearing in an excerpt from *Separate Tables* as part of a charity performance tribute to the newly-knighted Terence Rattigan.

In 1973 Trevor was among an all-star cast in *Craze*, in which the emphasis was on shock. Or some might think, laughs. Trevor certainly did:

> I'd never done a horror picture before, so I thought I'd have a go when Freddie Francis [the director] asked me to be in it. It was really great fun. I mean, there was Jack Palance as intense as ever playing this crazy antiques dealer offering sacrifices to some nasty African god or whatever it was, and there was no way you could take it seriously.

Trevor was in good company. Diana Dors, Edith Evans, Hugh Griffith, Michael Jayston, Suzy Kendall and all the other performers had a ball. The film itself may not have been exactly great cinema, but it was very commercial and free of the kind of problems that beset a good many of the more prestigious films Trevor had been associated with.

In July of that year Trevor attended the San Sebastian film festival and met up with a good friend of his, newspaper show biz columnist William Hall. Fifty miles away from San Sebastian, Pamplona was preparing for its annual run with the bulls as part of the week-long San Fernin Fiesta. The run, spread over three-quarters of a mile, is for anyone brave (or crazy) enough to try and keep one step ahead of eight fighting bulls as the beasts enjoy their last stampede before meeting their fate in the bull ring.

Bill Hall had enjoyed numerous occasions with Trevor on location when a few too many drinks had got the better of them, but this proved to be one of Hall's and Trevor's most memorable encounters: Trevor suddenly announced that he was going to run with the bulls, and asked Hall to join him in this adventure. 'I'm not trying to prove anything,' declared Trevor. 'I'm just trying to do it all.'

'He was then 56, with 15 years still to go,' said William Hall, 'but you could sense the rage for living boiling up inside him – or perhaps the fear of not living life to the hilt.'

'I've always lived on borrowed time, amigo,' Trevor told him. 'You must never lose sight of adventure in your life. I've always wanted to be an explorer – but today there's very little that hasn't been done. But,' he cried thumping the table and making the glasses jump, 'I've lived a fantastic life. And there aren't so many people who can say that.'

A few hours later they were making the two-hour drive through the foothills of the Pyrenees, 'bolstered,' said Bill Hall, 'by copious quantities of vodka and clamato juice, which is one up on a Bloody Mary.' In the early hours of the morning they found themselves, far from sober, standing in Pamplona's main square. Here they waited for the town hall clock to strike 7 a.m. when eight bulls and four angry cows would be let loose to race through the narrow streets that were boarded with railway sleepers to protect those who preferred to watch rather than to race along with them.

Trevor and William Hall began wondering if they were not perhaps just a little insane. 'We must be mad doing this,' said Trevor. 'But what's the good of sitting at home and never taking a risk?'

There were 2,000 other would-be runners around them waiting for the clock to chime. At 7 a.m. a cannon fired, signalling the start. The brave and generally drunken crowd of runners moved off at a slow trot up the street, knowing that soon the bulls would be let loose, and 100,000 spectators, safe behind the barriers or clinging to walls and balconies for a better view, urged them on.

Anyone who began the run was expected to finish. No one was allowed to leap behind the safety of the barriers. Police stood by ready with truncheons to make sure the tradition of the fiesta was not broken. Bill Hall saw one man, who suddenly decided he wanted to quit, forced back by a policeman who shouted, 'You are in the run, señor, so run.' There was almost a state of hysteria among the runners, and Trevor and Bill Hall felt that danger could come not just from the rampaging bulls but also from the crowd if panic suddenly swept through them. 'My God,' panted Trevor trotting alongside Bill Hall, 'I didn't think it would be like this.'

Then came the thunder of the second cannon, signalling the release of the bulls from a railway yard. Trevor, Hall and everyone else began running faster, cheered on by the onlookers. 'The big danger,' explained Bill Hall, 'is that someone at the front looks back, trips on the cobbles, and 50 people pile up on him. Because once those bulls start running, they don't stop. The previous year, two people had been killed outright in a threshing pile before the bulls even got to the stadium.'

Trevor, all out of puff, slowed to a walk and stared back. Hall urged him on.

'I see no bulls,' Trevor declared.

'They're there,' shouted Hall 'so run, Trevor, run.' But Trevor wasn't running. Hall grabbed his arm and tugged him forwards. A policeman leaned over the barrier, thumping it with his baton, shouting to Trevor and Bill, 'Quick *señors*, the *toros* are right behind.'

Suddenly the bulls came thundering round the corner and people began leaping over barriers past the policemen or up onto overhanging balconies. At the sight of the bulls Trevor said softly, 'Good God!' and decided he was going to ignore the police and get through the nearest make-shift barrier. But he got his leg caught between two planks of wood and was stuck there. Bill dived to the ground, rolling under the barrier in a manoeuvre he called 'saving your own skin'.

Fortunately the bulls came careering down the other side of the street, missing Trevor, still stuck fast in the barricade, by yards. Had they come running down his side of the street he would have been trampled on. All around, those who had dived to the ground or been mown down were picking themselves up, dusting themselves off and congratulating each other on their courage. Trevor managed to free his leg. Then he and Bill, both shaken and now stone-cold sober, stumbled over to Hemingway's café in the main square.

Trevor called for vodka and was besieged by people who suddenly recognised him. He signed autographs, and he and Bill Hall knocked back a couple of vodkas. Then Trevor suddenly realised what he'd done: his famous roar was heard all over the square as he cried, 'Fan-bloody-tastic! I played the game, didn't I?'

'You did, amigo,' said Bill Hall. Not surprisingly, Bill never forgot it. And he lived to tell the tale.

15

A Wonderful Life

ALTHOUGH FILM PRODUCERS rarely came up with really superior roles for Trevor to play, he could always count on American television to offer something other than the usual typecast parts. One such part was the abbot in the excellent futuristic religious drama *Catholics* for CBS-TV in 1973. It also starred Martin Sheen and Cyril Cusack and, although it didn't win any Emmys, it was highly praised by the Press when it aired on the CBS network in 1974. *The New York Times* said, in particular, 'Trevor Howard's abbot is nothing short of magnificent.'

Then it was back to the inevitable supporting film role, this time in another so-called shocker, *Persecution*, filmed late in 1973 at Pinewood. It was certainly shocking, but not in the way the director Don Chaffey intended. Hollywood legend Lana Turner, then aged 52 and still stunning, starred as an embittered woman, crippled by her former lover. Her son, and that of her lover, played in his adult years by Ralph Bates, is persecuted by his mother, who manages, with the help of her cat Sheba, to bring about the death of his wife and baby.

Trevor appears only briefly as Turner's former lover, but there are one or two glimpses of his younger self when Ralph Bates finds photographs of him taken in earlier days. He must have been thankful to have been so mercifully excluded from the bulk of this film which was produced by Kevin Francis, son of Freddie Francis. Even Lana Turner publicly labelled the film 'a bomb', and when I asked Ralph Bates about the film he said, 'Well, it paid for my new carpet.'

Said Trevor, 'The film was an opportunity to make a little money, play a role that in itself wasn't bad and I got to work with a real live sex symbol, which hasn't happened often in my career. No, I didn't get to know her much.

139

There wasn't a lot of time for that sort of thing. My role
was very small and they were shooting on a shoe-string
and the film was being shot very fast. I don't know, but I
suspect the most expensive item in their budget was Miss
Turner's wardrobe.'

In the hope of something more rewarding, Trevor took to
treading the boards for the first time in 10 years (with the
exception of the excerpt from *Separate Tables* in 1972) and
starred in *The Waltz Of The Toreadors* at the Haymarket
Theatre in February 1974. To see him once again on the stage
was a long-awaited opportunity. But it was a let down, not
least for Trevor. On the opening night he was suffering from a
sore throat and his performance was noticeably hampered.
Although the throat cleared up, he remained subdued
throughout the run. He had suspected that the theatre had
lost its magic for him, and when he finished the play he felt he
ought perhaps to stick to films and TV, hoping to find the
occasional gem. If he had to act for a living, he would keep on
doing it for as long as he could – or as long as he was asked to.

That year, in July, his mother died. She was in her nineties
although no one knew for sure exactly how old she was.

That same year he was one of the cameos in *Eleven
Harrowhouse*, a 'caper' movie which featured a double-cross by
Trevor, treachery by James Mason and some light relief from
John Gielgud. It all proved more entertaining than the actual
point of the film which was the theft of diamonds worth
billions of dollars by Charles Grodin.

If Trevor seems not to have been particularly selective at
this stage of his career, he maintained that he always tried to
find something of value in the films he did. Of *Eleven
Harrowhouse*, he said, 'It actually read bloody well as a script.
Really quite amusing. But the director [Aram Avakian] didn't
seem to know what to do with it. It was just a muddle. It also
had a part in it for Helen which made it fun for me. But if it
was a mistake to do the film, then the mistake was made by
James Mason and John Gielgud too, so I'm in good company,
amigo!'

The offers kept coming. There wasn't always much to
choose from, but the script for *Conduct Unbecoming* looked

promising. It was based on a successful West End court-room
production set against the military rule of India in the 1890s.
But under the direction of Michael Anderson, whose
craftsmanship always outweighed his inspiration, it failed to
capture any real sense of the period. Its strong point was a fine
cast – Michael York, Stacy Keach, Christopher Plummer,
Richard Attenborough, Susannah York and, of course, Trevor
– but it was destined never to reach a wide audience.

Then, in 1975, he turned up in the unfortunate *Hennessy* in
which Rod Steiger planned to blow up the Royal Family –
unfortunate because actual newsreel footage of the Royals was
used and, judging it was in rather poor taste at a time when
IRA bombings in Britain were becoming more frequent, the
film was refused a release by both the major British cinema
circuits.

That same year Trevor made *The Bawdy Adventures Of Tom
Jones*, a musical version of Henry Fielding's tale of the randy
18th-century lad who had been immortalised on screen in
Tony Richardson's 1963 classic *Tom Jones*. The new version
was based on a Las Vegas stage production, and with
inevitable comparisons made with Richardson's film, it
couldn't hope to win any critical kudos. Which is a shame
because it actually isn't as bad as you might think. It had at
least three good musical numbers and a strong cast including
Nicky Henson in the title role, Joan Collins as highwaywoman
Black Bess, Arthur Lowe and Terry-Thomas. Trevor played
the squire who discovers Tom as a baby in his bed and brings
him up as his illegitimate son. Said Trevor:

> It was obvious going in that the film was going to be
> knocked, but you can't keep making films to please the
> critics. I knew it would be commercial, especially with all
> the randy goings-on that could be portrayed more freely
> than when Tony Richardson made *Tom Jones*. And the
> squire was a fun part. Those don't come along often. It's
> fun to be outrageous every now and then. And these little
> English films that you know are never going to be taken ·
> seriously are almost without exception fun to make. You
> don't get the big movie stars giving . . . well you know,
> amigo – hell!'

After this Trevor went to Rhodesia to film *Death In The Sun* with Christopher Lee – a film which has never surfaced.

I can remember how, towards the end of my conversation with Trevor, he became quite defensive about his frequent appearances in films during the Seventies.

Look, old boy, there are two trains of thought about acting. One is that you can sit on your backside and wait for just the right part or the right film to land on your lap. And that's what I did earlier in my life. Today if I tried to do that I'd never work. And the other is that you can take what comes along and not expect every film you make to be the greatest you'll ever do.

Too many actors worry themselves to death about getting old and no longer getting the plum parts. Now look at me, I'm over 60, so they're not going to want me for a leading man, are they? And I'm glad I'm not young in today's cinema. If I were I'd be lucky to get any work these days. There just aren't as many films being made as there were in my era, old son, so there are fewer parts on offer. But I get to do a lot of films. Some of them occasionally turn out quite well, and I don't have to spend two or three months making each one, so I can make a few films a year, and they pay me well so I won't go broke just yet.

It's my own fault, amigo. I chose to become an actor, and now I'm stuck with it. Like you. If you don't want to be a newspaper man all your life, you have to change direction soon or it will probably be too late. Well, I left it too late to do anything else long ago. But there again, I've loved every minute of it. What's that film with Jimmy Stewart? *It's A Wonderful Life*. That's me, amigo. I'm really Jimmy Stewart in *It's A Wonderful Life*. You see, Mike, I always knew it was a wonderful life, all along, but every now and then you get bogged down and you wonder about it all. But today I can look back and know it. I've done it, for God's sake. I've lived a wonderful life.

He stopped and thought for a moment, taking a sip of beer, and added, 'I sound like an epitaph.'

With so much money from so much work, it seemed that he ought to do something with it. So in 1975 he and Helen bought a villa in the South of France. It became a home away from home where Trevor and Helen spent more time in each other's company than they probably did in England. At home in Arkley Trevor was more likely to go off and watch cricket and Helen was often out pursuing her own particular interests. But they could never conceive of actually living in France. To them Arkley was their home, and they had no intention of exiling themselves in Europe. Although that may have looked the case that year when newspaper headlines began screaming that Trevor Howard was facing a charge of income tax evasion.

Where the story originated isn't clear, but as it didn't contain a shred of truth Trevor decided to have fun with it and announced he was close to bankruptcy. The newspapers printed his admission of serious financial misconduct, only to discover later that not only was he extremely solvent but the Inland Revenue were bringing no such charges against him. Trevor just sat back and chuckled. Typically, he had told the Press exactly what they had wanted to hear and it ultimately amused him far more than it did them.

That same year producer Norman Rosemont came up with a role for Trevor that he couldn't resist. It had to be the most unglamorous role of his career, dressed in dirty rags and his face virtually hidden by long matted hair and a flea-ridden beard. It was for a TV film of Alexandre Dumas' *The Count Of Monte Cristo*, one of the most-filmed novels of all time. No less than 14 screen versions have been derived from the story of dashing Edmond Dantes who is unjustly imprisoned by his enemies and escapes to discover the fabulous treasure on Monte Cristo.

Richard Chamberlain was an admirable Dantes, but once again it was Trevor who came away with honours, receiving an Emmy nomination for his performance as the old prisoner Abbé Faria whom Dantes meets in prison and from whom he learns the secret of the treasure. As a TV film it was lavish, romantic and exciting, but in the UK it was acquired for cinema release by Scotia-Barber film distributors, and on the big screen the inevitable flaws of a TV movie showed up, not to mention the obvious cues for commercial breaks. It looked a grand production on the box but somehow cheap on a cinema screen.

And because Trevor's role was confined to one segment of the film involving scenes only with Chamberlain, he didn't even get to meet half the impressive line-up of stars which included Tony Curtis, Donald Pleasence, Kate Nelligan and Louis Jourdan.

As if he hadn't already made enough films in 1975, he also made *Kidnapped*. In this film he renewed his acquaintance with Michael Caine who had the star part of Alan Breck, the outlaw of Robert Louis Stevenson's book about 18th-century Scotland. It also featured his old friend Jack Hawkins who continued to work with the aid of fellow actors like Charles Gray who could adequately dub his voice in.

Unfortunately Trevor didn't get to share a scene with either Hawkins or Caine, performing in only a few scenes as the Lord Advocate. He appeared mainly with Lawrence Douglas as the young kidnapped David. It was an extremely fraught production: half-way through filming the money ran out. Delbert Mann, the director, desperately tried to coax everyone into getting on with the film, even though there was a real threat no one would ever get paid. The stuntmen, without whom the film couldn't possibly be made because of all the swashbuckling action, rebelled, and Michael Caine joined with Mann in placating them and getting them back to work. Trevor was one of the lucky cameos: he was not around long enough to get caught up in all this turmoil. But what did affect Trevor was that, as everyone had feared, no one was ever fully paid.

Trevor was typecast again in *Aces High* in 1976. It was a well-made statement on the wastefulness of war, focusing on the sacrifices of young pilots in World War One. Starring Malcolm McDowell, Christopher Plummer, Simon Ward and Peter Firth, the film had four cameo stars of which one was Trevor. The others were John Gielgud, Ray Milland and Richard Johnson.

After this Trevor went to Australia to film *Eleven Harrowhouse*. Whenever he could, Trevor always took time to promote his films. He said:

> It's all part of the job. You always find some actors who say 'I got paid only for making the film, so let the studio publicise it.' But I've always thought that actors are the best resource a film company has to publicise a film. Besides, if you want the public to come and see you as often as they'll tolerate you, you must make the effort to do more than just make films you'll hope the public will like. You must promote them.
>
> I remember when Rank were promoting *Brief Encounter*. They didn't figure anyone was interested in me, so they sent Celia on a publicity tour and I was never asked to join her. They didn't even invite me to the bloody press show. So I thought 'Right, if they won't give me an invitation, I'll gate crash the bloody thing.' And I did. I just turned up.

During the spring of 1976 he and Helen returned to Australia where he was to appear in *Eliza Fraser* with Susannah York in the title role. Director Tim Burstall had initially asked Trevor if he'd like to play the male lead. The film appealed to Trevor but he had no intention of missing the cricket he'd planned to see while in Australia, so he asked for a smaller role and got it.

Trevor had more or less decided that he'd finished with the theatre when both he and Helen received an offer to do *The Scenario* by Anouilh in Canada at the end of 1976. They'd had little enough chance to work together so they both accepted. Christmas of that year saw them in Toronto performing together at the Royal Alexandra Theatre. But it basically confirmed what Trevor already knew in his heart. He was through with theatre.

Meanwhile, in Hollywood, a new director had come onto the scene who had a perfectly brilliant idea of making a movie that would send up the old Universal swashbucklers. He was British comic Marty Feldman who started out as a comedy writer for British TV and became a TV star in his own right in 1967. He'd made his film début in 1969 in *The Bed Sitting Room*, then had his own starring vehicle in *Every Home Should Have One*, and was brought to Hollywood by mad-cap Mel Brooks in 1974 to feature in *Young Frankenstein*. After a couple more movies he wrote his own screenplay of *The Last Remake Of Beau Geste* and convinced Universal to let him direct it in 1977. In a moment of inspired lunacy he cast himself and Michael York as twin brothers! He also enlisted – reluctantly it would seem – stars like Ann-Margret, Peter Ustinov, James Earl Jones, Spike Milligan, Terry-Thomas, Roy Kinnear, Hugh Griffith, Irene Handl and Trevor Howard. In the role of Sir Hector Geste, Trevor, by now obviously wary of expensive Hollywood films, had a wonderful time. Besides, he didn't even have to go to Hollywood. His scenes were shot in Dublin, while the rest of the film was shot on location in Spain.

'Working with Marty Feldman was great fun,' Trevor told me. 'I think perhaps he was undisciplined as a director but in a sense that was all part of his – well, I was going to say genius, but that's too strong a word. But he had a vision.' Actually, Marty had wanted to make his film in Hollywood. 'What I really wanted to do,' he'd said, 'was a very simple back lot picture that looked like a back lot picture. I wanted everyone to look like Maria Montez and Jon Hall. Instead, I wound up with a huge budget with big stars.'

Universal didn't have quite the same vision as Feldman and were intent on pouring almost six million dollars into it. So Feldman had no choice but to spend their money. 'I don't know if Marty could have actually made the film he had in mind the way he wanted,' said Trevor, 'but I don't think it helped him having so much money at his disposal. He said to me, "We've got all this money so let's be extravagant", but really I think he would have preferred to have it look like a cheap 1950s picture, which after all was the whole joke to start with.'

If the whole enterprise was being turned into an expensive party, then all concerned seemed determined to enjoy the party. Trevor was working closely with two brilliant comics, Marty Feldman and Spike Milligan who played Trevor's elderly servant. 'It was wonderful to wake up in the morning and go to work,' he said, 'because I knew I was going to laugh all day. You can't not laugh with Marty Feldman and Spike Milligan around you all the time. They were so inventive and spontaneous there was a very real danger of straying from the story line, but it was great fun. But perhaps not the best way to make a movie.'

Universal obviously weren't that overwhelmed with the picture Marty gave them: they re-cut it and the version that went out in 1978 was not, Marty Feldman claimed, his version.

During 1977 Trevor went off to Africa to star in *Slavers*, a German-made drama about slave-trading in 19th-century Africa. The conditions were nowhere near as primitive as they had been when he first went to Africa to do *The Roots Of Heaven* with Errol Flynn. The cast, including Ron Ely (TV's Tarzan), Britt Ekland and Ray Milland, stayed in a comfortable hotel. Trevor enjoyed Milland's company during the evenings in the bar, the two of them probably wondering how to make sense of the second-rate script they were working from. Ray Milland once told me:

> I made this awful film called *Slavers* a couple of years ago and Trevor Howard was in it who I always thought was a marvellous actor who usually made very good films, and after about a week into the picture I said to him, 'Look, Trevor, just why are you making this picture which we all know is going to be awful?' And he said, 'I was wondering why *you're* doing it.' Neither of us could figure out what each other was doing in it, and thankfully I don't think the film's ever been shown.

In October 1977 Trevor returned to Hollywood to film the few scenes he had in *Meteor* – a film coming at the end of the 'disaster films' cycle and the beginning of the resurrected sci-fi genre which began (arguably perhaps) with *Star Wars*. Directed by Ronald Neame, who had really kicked off the 'disaster genre' with *The Poseidon Adventure* six years earlier, this was a film about a giant meteor on collision course with earth, filled with some rather shoddy special effects and lots of star names.

Sean Connery, Natalie Wood and Karl Malden were the main stars and Trevor was just another cameo, as was Henry Fonda as the American president. The film was a waste of Trevor's talent: he had nothing much more to do than report on Great Britain's wellbeing as fragments of the meteor began pounding the earth. There were some moments of real suspense, but in a day and age when there are no excuses for poor special effects (except perhaps for lack of money) this film was let down badly by unconvincing scenes of avalanches and tidal waves.

In 1978 Trevor finally returned to British TV screens when he starred in *Easterman*. It was the first of six plays in the series *Scorpion Tales*. Each tale had a different cast and a different subject, but common to all was the element of terror. In *Easterman*, Trevor played CID Inspector Mavor investigating a savage attack on one of his young officers and finding himself the potential victim of a maniac killer.

'It seems that television is the one medium where I can almost always find something that I feel is really worthwhile,' he said. 'But then I don't do as much TV as I do films – for the cinema that is.'

That same year Trevor made three films, two of them expensive super-productions with all the usual commercial trimmings while the other was a more modest enterprise. This film, *Stevie*, could hardly hope to compete in the commercial market and yet he felt it was far superior to the others. Based on Hugh Whitemore's London stage play about the British poetess Stevie Smith, Glenda Jackson had the title role and Trevor played The Man, a character symbolic of Stevie's literary friends. Trevor told me:

It was a wonderful little film that I don't suppose too many people went to see, but they should have because Glenda Jackson was so superb in it. I remember when we did *Mary Queen Of Scots* I said to her one day, 'There has got to be a better script than this we can do together one day,' and *Stevie* was it.

It was a film that had to be shot quickly because Glenda was involved in a play or something, and so it was all a bit rushed which is okay if you're not aiming for something special, but I think we all felt this was. But because the play itself was so good and Glenda such a professional and excellent actress, it all worked exceptionally well and I felt very proud to be in it. Mind you, it was a bit abstract for me. I never really knew quite what I was supposed to be doing.

What he was supposed to be doing was playing the link-man between the film and the audience.

Then it was off to Bora Bora for *Hurricane*, a remake of the 1937 Samuel Goldwyn classic famous for Dorothy Lamour's legs and a spectacular climax as the hurricane hits a South Pacific island. This new version, like *Meteor*, was made to cash in on the trend in disaster epics which were, however, by now boring the public. Italian showman Dino De Laurentiis poured $22 million into this lavish production, bringing his cast, including Jason Robards, Mia Farrow, Max, von Sydow and Timothy Bottoms, and unit to live in a specially built hotel on the island of Bora Bora for several months. Such was the extravagance of the whole enterprise.

Helen came with Trevor and it proved to be a holiday paradise for her. The sun and sea were warm and the locals hospitable. Said Trevor, 'I had a lot of time to spare while *Hurricane* was being filmed so we went off to explore the island which wasn't much. Just a Chinese store, a rock and the Club Mediterranée – that's all there was there.' And for Trevor it must also have brought memories of filming *Mutiny On The Bounty* flooding back with the surf.

Dino De Laurentiis, a surprisingly tiny man for such a giant in the cinema, was constantly on the set. His past experience of overseeing mammoth productions was the result of making films like *War And Peace*, *Barabbas* and *The Bible In The Beginning*. He never skimped on budgets and he wanted his director, Jan Troell, to pull out all the stops with the spectacle. But Troell did more than that. One of Sweden's leading directors, he had a typically Swedish approach: if the film fails, like *Meteor*, in the special effects department, it succeeds more in telling a sensitive love story between an American girl, played by Mia Farrow, and an islander, played by Dayton Ka'ne.

But, like *Meteor*, it was a film that came too late. The public
had had enough of films like *The Towering Inferno* and
Earthquake. In fact, throughout the Seventies, film attendances
had consistently fallen and only the passing trends, the James
Bond movies, Clint Eastwood and, to a lesser extent, Charles
Bronson, usually guaranteed pulling them in. Films released
on video cassettes were starting to keep people at home.
Which is why producers were so keen to jump on the
bandwagons that came rolling by – and both *Meteor* and
Hurricane were among the casualties that fell off with loud and
expensive bumps that were more spectacularly disastrous for
the industry than the events they portrayed on the screen.

As for the British film industry, it was all but gone, revived
from time to time, as it continues to be, but to all intents and
purposes little more than a rental agency for some of the more
successful American-made films like *Star Wars* and its sequels,
and the Indiana Jones films (all of which have helped keep the
British film studios open). Such films began bringing
audiences back to the cinema, proving that it's best to let the
bandwagons pass by and come up with something more
original in style if not in concept.

Part of the resurgence of the British film industry was the
colossal success of *Superman – The Movie*. Like the *Star Wars*
series, *Superman* and most of its sequels were filmed in English
studios, in this case Pinewood. A great deal of interest
surrounded the acquisition of Marlon Brando to appear in the
opening scenes, and it was easy to ignore the fact that a
newcomer called Christopher Reeve had the title role, and
that other members of the cast included Susannah York, Ned
Beatty, Gene Hackman, Harry Andrews, Jackie Cooper,
Margot Kidder and Trevor Howard.

It's ironic that the one actor Trevor hoped never to work
with again was Marlon Brando, yet this, his third film with
Brando, required them both to appear in the opening scenes
on the planet Krypton, just prior to its destruction. How the
producers Ilya and Alexander Salkind and Pierre Spengler
managed to coerce Trevor into doing *Superman*, I don't know,
but Patrick Newell told me, 'He said he would do *Superman* as
long as he didn't have to act with Brando.'

On screen it certainly looks as though the two were kept

separate. Trevor, playing one of the elders of Krypton, appears in the opening scene as a large projected image (as was Harry Andrews), while Brando was actually on the sound stage, prosecuting three villains (who turn up in *Superman II*). But Harry Andrews told me, 'We were on the set with Brando and I don't think Trevor was at all pleased about it.'

Much of the publicity surrounding Brando's involvement was to do with the report that he was being paid an astronomical amount of money for his cameo – a reputed £2,250,000. 'Trevor was quite sickened by the sum Brando was being paid,' said Andrews, 'especially as Brando couldn't seem to remember his lines and had to read his dialogue off of boards.' And Trevor had never forgiven Brando, not so much for the troubles caused during the filming of *Mutiny On The Bounty*, but for tricking him into appearing in *Morituri*. Not surprisingly then, this was to be no warm reunion and Trevor steered clear of Brando altogether.

'I always thought no one got on with Brando,' said Trevor, 'but apparently Susannah York seemed to like him. I can get on with most people but him . . . Please, don't mention him again. I'm enjoying this chat, so ask me about something I like. Like cricket.'

I never did talk to him too much about cricket as I've never been keen on the sport (an oversight in life he seemed willing to forgive me for), but I did listen attentively as he went on at some length about people I've never heard of, who'd scored so many runs and bowled out so many batsmen. But through it all I couldn't help but come away with the feeling that here was a man trapped by his own early ambition to be an actor when he would have really preferred to have been out in front of the stumps at Lord's, scoring a hundred runs for England.

When he asked me if I played or watched cricket, I admitted I didn't. 'Oh!' he sighed. 'Better stick to films then, old boy. I can talk about them as well.'

16

So Well Remembered?

In 1979 Trevor went to Montreal to film *Night Flight*, a 30-minute telemovie. Directed by Desmond Davis, it was set in the 1930s with Trevor playing a veteran pilot in charge of a fleet of French planes flying mail over the wilds of South America. Bo Svenson played a pilot who becomes lost in a storm during a night flight, and Canadian actress Celine Lomez played his wife. A number of Trevor's scenes were with the pilot's wife, waiting anxiously on the ground. Of Trevor, Celine Lomez said, 'It's lovely working with Trevor – like a waltz with a great partner. He carries you.'

Again he won rave reviews; Terence Pettigrew discovered just how proud Trevor was of his good notices when he thrust one into Terence's hands which read, 'Howard was never better as the hard-bitten veteran who would much rather be in the plane than on the ground waiting.'

There now came a shift in Trevor's career. He began appearing less in multimillion-dollar all-star productions and chose instead to work more in television and smaller films that offered him much more in the way of roles other than the major supporting cameos. Consequently, during the last decade of his life he did some of his best screen work.

Around this time he was keen to play the role of Adolf Eichmann in a filmed reconstruction of his war-crimes trial. The script had been offered to him. He'd read it and considered it 'really thoughtful', and he was on line for what could have been an important leading role. Helen, mindful of Trevor's ability to play for warmth so convincingly, said to him, 'If you play Eichmann, you'll finish up with everyone on your side.' That in itself was a compliment which touched Trevor deeply, and it was to his great disappointment that the whole project was scrapped.

Then along came *The Shillingbury Blowers*, a full-length feature film for British television. Again it offered him something different – a leading role playing against type as Old Saltie, the conductor of the Shillingbury Brass Band. The story centres around a quiet English village where the local brass band finds itself in competition with the arrival of a pop musician. It was hardly thrilling stuff but, as a gentle throwback to the days of the Ealing comedies, it was intended by its producer Greg Smith as a pilot for a regular TV series. This meant that Trevor had an opportunity many actors dream of – being a TV star in a regular series. But he didn't want it. 'I don't want to get bored with playing the same part,' he told me. 'That's almost like doing a play for months on end, only this could run into years.'

The younger members of the cast held Trevor in very high esteem. Robin Nedwell said:

> It's a privilege to work with Trevor. He is one of the greats of British cinema, isn't he? I'm just a newcomer compared to him and that in itself can seem a daunting prospect because it's easy to think that maybe this movie star is going to come in and hog the whole thing. But Trevor isn't like that. He gives you everything you need, and a whole lot you may not think you need. Being a good actor isn't all about pretending to be somebody else; it's also a matter of generosity to the people you work with, and, of course, I can learn a great deal from him. I think I can say with pride that I have worked with Trevor Howard.

And Diane Keen said:

> It sounds almost an outdated thing to say, but he is the perfect gentleman, which is something we must value in this day and age. He treats a lady like a lady, although I notice he seems to prefer the company of men. He has some old friends of his in this film, like Patrick Newell, and I've seen them go off to the pub together for a pint and a chat. I gather they're both keen on cricket. And I think for him this is a happy picture to work on, which I

gather has not always been the case with some of the films he has made. But then I suppose when you've made as many films as he has, there are bound to be a few that had problems. He's clever, he can be funny, and I don't suppose there is anything we can teach him.

I remember Patrick telling me, 'At least on this one there are no great egos to contend with, or perhaps I should say vanity because all actors have a certain ego, but vanity can be destructive. Trevor isn't vain.'

Greg Smith told me, 'You can't underestimate the value of a star like Trevor Howard in this really very moderately budgeted film. All the rest of our cast mainly come from television, but Trevor is of the old school of film actors, when film actors were film stars. I'm sure he can teach the others a thing or two. And he is so accommodating. He doesn't have the slightest sign of a temperament.'

Working for the first time with Trevor was director Val Guest who said of him, 'As an actor he gives you what you ask for, and more, and no director can ask more of an actor. I'm not surprised the David Leans and the Carol Reeds always ask for him.'

The only person I ever heard speak of Trevor Howard in lesser terms was the man himself who told me:

Look, amigo, it's very gratifying to be appreciated, but I am human after all and I have my failings like you do. Like everyone has. I can lose my temper. Have done a number of times. Not for the sake of being bad tempered though. And I've never punched anyone. Nearly have. Or felt like it. I don't see any point in being unpleasant like some people seem to. We all have to live in this world, and for actors in particular I think it's important that we all get on otherwise it only affects the work we're being paid very nicely to do. But I can be mean if I want to.

And I can get drunk. I can get roaring drunk. I can make a lot of noise. But please don't say I raise hell. Errol Flynn could raise hell. Ollie Reed can raise hell. I don't.

You know, if there are two things that have plagued me throughout much of my career, they are being called a hellraiser and being asked about Marlon Brando. I'd like to think I'd be remembered for more than those two single things. So dammit, yes, it's bloody nice when people say 'Trevor's a fine chap and a good actor'. But when I eventually snuff it the papers are going to say, 'He was a hellraiser'. You'll probably write that I am. I only hope that I might be remembered for some of the good work which I think I've done.

I assured him he would. But maybe he felt that after so many years making films, of which so few were really memorable, he was in danger of being overlooked as a serious actor. And to some extent I think in the public's eye that may be true. To a good many people he was a lovable British actor with a penchant for drinking who was said to raise hell. That image alone kept his name more vividly alive in people's memories than the titles of his films, very few of which seem to linger in the mind, except that of the more avid filmgoer. Almost everyone can name *Brief Encounter*, but few others. And that was something Trevor dreaded. He said, 'I'd hate to think I'd only ever be remembered for *Brief Encounter*.' Or for being a hellraiser; or for working with Marlon Brando.

Fortunately, film buffs and actors and those with more than a general interest in the cinema and the theatre are not ignorant of the substantial contribution Trevor Howard made to his profession. They are well aware that his performances have more often than not been superior to the films he was in. And in the theatre it was only his declining ambition that prevented him from becoming a really great classical actor. If there was one fault Trevor Howard had, it was his attitude. He set out to become a successful actor, which at the time meant working in the theatre, but in the end he lacked heart for it. And as for being a film star, he never really had the kind of looks that would count him among the likes of Ronald Colman, George Sanders or David Niven, and yet he was undoubtedly a far better actor than any of these. What he eventually became was a great character actor, but one who rarely found the great character roles to play.

Perhaps if it hadn't been for the fact that he liked to 'live life to the full', he might have quit the profession years ago.

Making films gave him the opportunity to live a lifestyle he enjoyed, and pursued with some zeal, though I wouldn't dare venture the use of the phrase 'with a vengeance', because he never went about it with any amount of ferocity or violence.

There was certainly nothing ferocious about the man I met down on the set of *The Shillingbury Blowers* and talked to for an hour or so in the pub.

'If you're coming down here again we'll talk some more,' said Trevor, rising from his chair. 'If not, maybe we'll meet on some other set. Or come to my home some day. Meet Helen, amigo.'

Well, I never did meet him again. I never got to go on any of his subsequent film sets and I certainly didn't feel presumptuous enough to go knocking at his front door, even though the invitation to do so seemed open enough. And it is at this point that I'd feel inclined to end this biography if only for the fact that from here on I cannot include anything Trevor said to me personally. But he did, in the last nine years of his life, go on to do some outstanding work, and if he should be remembered for more than *Brief Encounter*, as he'd hoped he would be, none of it should be excluded.

17

A Few Risks

ODDLY ENOUGH, DURING the last nine years of his life
Trevor's interest in acting seemed to be revived. He did fewer
cameos than usual and took greater gambles in films that
offered him superior roles but really had few hopes of ever
proving commercial. Perhaps by this time he felt he had little
to lose. He could afford to turn down the bread-and-butter
parts and take a few risks.

He was on British TV in 1979, repeating a sequence from
The Recruiting Officer ('The play that brought Helen into my
life') in the series *Words On War*. The following year he was
reunited with Celia Johnson in the TV play *Staying On*, filmed
in India. According to his agent Marina Martin, he said it was
a case of 'déjà vu'. It was his first professional reunion with
Celia Johnson and, thrilled as he was about that, he was
disappointed not to have worked with Dame Wendy Hiller.
She was originally to have played Celia's role, and in fact had
persuaded Trevor to do the play in the first place. When
Dame Wendy had to drop out due to other commitments,
Granada TV offered the part to Celia Johnson. She
immediately decided she didn't want to go to India, but was
eventually persuaded to do so.

So the two stars were at long last brought together again,
both after persuasion, and the result, under the direction
of Silvio Narizzano, was a beautiful tale of bygone days in
India. Both stars gave exceptional performances that brought
waves of nostalgia flooding back for another bygone age – the
era of *Brief Encounter*. It did seem that Trevor was never totally
going to escape the shadow of the film that made him
famous.

In India again in 1980, Trevor was filming *The Sea Wolves*.
Produced by Euan Lloyd and directed by Andrew V.
McLaglen, this was something of a follow-up to *The Wild*

Geese, which had proved a huge success for Lloyd and McLaglen in 1978. Reginald Rose, who had scripted *The Wild Geese,* wrote the screenplay for *The Sea Wolves,* based on the novel *Boarding Party* by James Leasor. It was the story of a territorial unit known as the Calcutta Light Horse who, in 1943, sabotaged a German attempt to broadcast from the neutral harbour of Goa in India.

Roger Moore, one of the stars of *The Wild Geese,* was recruited and, at 51 years of age, proved to be one of the younger members of a cast of 'veterans' in a film one London critic called 'Golden Oldies Go To War'. At the invitation of his old friend Euan Lloyd, Trevor Howard, then 63, took one of the leading roles. Gregory Peck, five months older than Trevor, and David Niven, who was just nudging 70, also took leading roles.

Taking the only female lead in this male-dominated war picture was Barbara Kellerman, then in her early thirties and a relative youngster. She told me:

> It was an exhausting film to make. Even Greg, David, Roger and Trevor who were used to difficult films said that this one was one of the most tiring. The heat was tremendous and sometimes got to 140 in the day. Everyone was ill. If it wasn't the runs it was flu. Most of my scenes were with Roger and he had to have eight shirts hanging on a line for him to change into because he just got soaked through with sweat. You couldn't drink the water so there was David and Trevor and all the men drinking various cocktails to keep them from getting dehydrated.

For a rare change in a recent large movie, Trevor had a major role and the rigours of filming in Goa proved exacting for him. He would rise at 7.30 a.m., as did the others, and filming often continued until 9 p.m. Filming usually ceased as mid-day approached because of the intense heat, and this gave everyone a chance to retire to the hotel for a leisurely drink. But no one could risk getting too drunk to continue filming later in the afternoon. By the end of a day's filming well into the evening there was no time for long drinking sessions. It was usually dinner and then bed, ready for the next early morning.

Trevor had only worked briefly with David Niven before, in *The Way Ahead* and *Around The World In Eighty Days*, but they were the kind of men who couldn't help but be good friends, and since Gregory Peck and Niven had been friends since they both starred in *The Guns Of Navarone*, and Roger Moore had always been one of the most amiable men in movies, the whole group was destined to become a close-knit ensemble. Trevor didn't know Greg Peck too well, but he grew to like him enormously, admitting Peck to the very selective and small group of American actors well liked by Trevor.

Having both formed friendships with Errol Flynn, Trevor and Niven swapped stories about the late Don Juan of Hollywood over a drink. But on the occasions when they sat up until late Trevor, like all the cast, was distressed to discover that Niven's voice began to slur. This had nothing to do with drinking alcohol; Niven was obviously ailing. His body ached and he was quickly exhausted. What nobody knew then was that David Niven was about to begin his three-year battle against the muscle-wasting illness known as 'Lou Gehrig's disease' which would eventually take his life.

Nevertheless, spirits were high throughout filming, and all came away with a sense of mutual admiration. As Roger Moore told me after he saw the film for the first time. 'David Niven, Trevor Howard and Gregory Peck are wonderful,' adding with typical self-derogatory humour, 'but there's this strange fellow called Roger Moore in it!'

From one extreme to the other, Trevor went from the heat of India to the snows of Utah for what has to be the most unusual role of his entire career, playing a Cheyenne warrior in *Windwalker*. It was the biggest surprise of his career when young American film director Keith Merill, looking for the 'best actor he could think of', offered him the role of Windwalker, an old Indian who dies and is resurrected to help his family fight their enemies, the Crow Indians. After reading the script Trevor described the role as 'a Red Indian King Lear'. He arrived with Helen in Salt Lake City to be greeted by Merill, a respected director who had won an Oscar for his documentary *The Great American Cowboy*. Merill was also a devout Mormon, and Trevor quickly realised that this was one director he couldn't expect to enjoy a binge with (as Mormons abstain from alcohol). News of the unusual partnership between the teetotal Merill and the hard-drinking Howard reached the British Press and one newspaper speculated on the chances of Trevor being converted to Mormonism. 'Trevor Howard a Mormon?' it asked incredulously.

But for Trevor there was no question of conversion and breaking the habit of a life-time. He did however stick to soft drinks while enjoying the hospitality of Merill's home. It was obviously going to be a relatively 'dry' location because, although alcohol can be purchased in Salt Lake City, it is as likely to produce unsettling stares from onlookers as buying a girlie magazine in the local newsagent.

Throughout the film Trevor narrates in English but his actual dialogue with the rest of the cast, which consisted totally of authentic Indians, had had to be spoken in Cheyenne. Intrigued and excited by this challenge, he underwent a crash course in the language, coached by a Professor of Indian Languages who himself was a full-blooded Cheyenne.

Merill took Trevor out to meet the Cheyenne tribe and the Navajos with whom he would be working, and he was given a warm welcome. He even discovered he had some fans among the Indians. Filming took place in the High Uintas mountains at an altitude of 12,000 feet. Trevor was required to wear contact lenses to turn his blue eyes brown, but he had to abandon them on the first day of filming: as he lay on a funeral pyre with the bright sun blazing down on him, the lenses began to cut into his corneas.

Making the film was an exhilarating and physically demanding experience as Trevor, then 63, had to wade through ice-packed rivers, ride a white stallion up and down snowy mountains, get chased by wolves and fight a full-grown grizzly bear. Marina Martin, Trevor's agent at that time, told me that the bear was playful enough but if annoyed was quite capable of skinning a man's face with one swipe. She told me Trevor's comment, 'Fortunately the bear and I got on terribly well. Actually, we had some very interesting conversations together!' It must have been an awesome sight: Trevor Howard with his long white hair, buffalo skin clothes, sitting on a rock of ice chatting with a bear, and stone-cold sober, too.

Marina Martin said that Trevor found *Windwalker* the most satisfying role of his career and he told her, 'It was pure hell but I wouldn't have missed it for the world.'

Unfortunately it proved a difficult commodity for its producers to sell for distribution. Praise was heaped upon it by critics. *The Monthly Film Bulletin* called it 'one of the year's five best films'. Other critics, both in the UK and the USA, thought the film deserving of Oscars for its photography, music score and Trevor's performance. But the film failed to classify for any Oscars because the Academy wouldn't consider it an American film, as it had a relatively non-English soundtrack, but neither would it accept it as a foreign film, because it was released just after the deadline for all foreign entrants.

Because it was an independently produced film, and particularly because it was so unusual, its producers Arthur R. Dubs and Thomas Ballard could find no major company to distribute it widely and they really needed at least one Oscar with which to sell it. It was a huge disappointment to Trevor who considered it one of his best films and one which he obviously hoped he might be remembered for.

Peculiarly, much of the best work of Trevor's last nine years has rarely been seen. After the initial exhilaration of making *Windwalker* and the subsequent disappointment of its failure to reach a wide audience, he starred in another highly regarded but little seen minor masterpiece, *Sir Henry At Rawlinson End*. It was based on the eccentric, alcoholic aristocrat created by Vivian Stanshall and featured on John Peel's Radio One show in 1977. Sir Henry became a cult character, later to be featured on a record album and then in a book. Stanshall collaborated with Steve Roberts on the screenplay for the film which Roberts directed in 1981.

Sir Henry At Rawlinson End was more of an enthusiastic semi-professional enterprise that probably had no real hope of ever being a commercial hit but could at best become a cult movie. Being a modest production it craved a star name to help sell it, but few important actors were likely to consider taking the lead role since, for one thing, the film's shoe-string budget of half a million dollars didn't offer much in the way of salary. But Trevor, when approached about it, saw the role itself as ample reward and decided he'd do it. This was somewhat to the consternation of Vivian Stanshall who thought Trevor ill-suited to play a character, by design a cross between Monty Python and Dylan Thomas.

But Trevor entered into the full spirit of the Stanshall creation, as for example in the scene where he sets about trying to exorcise a family ghost from his domain, and ultimately Stanshall had to agree that nobody could have played Sir Henry as superbly as Trevor. The final result, filmed in just three weeks in black and white and running little longer than an hour, was highly favoured by critics and Sir Henry enthusiasts.

Perhaps the film would have suited television much better and would most certainly have reached a more substantial audience which, after all, is surely what every actor craves. Trevor's next role did just that. He portrayed Jonathan Swift in BBC 2's *No Country For Old Men*. This was one of a handful of TV productions which, noted *The Times*, 'have brought Howard to our small screen with gratifying regularity and consistent distinction'.

The fact that his best work was now coming from all quarters except the British film industry was not lost on *The Times*. In 1981 it stated in its review of his next film, *Light Years Away*, that his 'vast gifts British films consistently squander'. *Light Years Away* was a curious piece – a Swiss-French co-production filmed in Ireland. Trevor played an old Russian immigrant, living in a petrol station, who meets a drifter (played by Mick Ford) and becomes his mentor. When he first read the screenplay he was baffled, but he thought the film was just the kind of risk he loved to take. Even after spending three months filming he never really understood it. However, his performance was duly appreciated by most critics and in 1982 he won the *Evening Standard*'s Best Actor award.

With nothing much to choose from in the way of British films, in 1982 Trevor travelled to Munich to spend two weeks portraying Professor Tessonow in an American cable TV film, *Inside The Third Reich,* an adaptation of Albert Speer's autobiography. Dutch actor Rutger Hauer starred as Speer and British actor Derek Jacobi gave a chilling portrayal of Hitler. The stellar line-up included John Gielgud, Maria Schell, Blythe Danner, Randy Quaid and Robert Vaughn. The two-part 250-minute film was very typical of the ambitious projects engineered for American TV – plenty of lavish detail but all rather jarringly adapted by screenwriter E. Jack Neuman and director Marvin J. Chomsky.

There followed another film for American cable, *The Deadly Game,* directed by George Schaefer, but this time in the BBC studios. Trevor received an Emmy nomination for his performance. He played one of four men who relive their former careers after rescuing a man (played by George Segal) lost in the Swiss snows whom they accuse of murdering his wife. Trevor was the prosecutor, Robert Morley the judge, Emlyn Williams the counsel for the defence and Alan Webb the hangman.

The year 1982 marked a welcome return to the British screens for Trevor in *Gandhi,* a film that was something of a landmark for British cinema. Once again he had little more than a cameo part, but it was one which director Richard Attenborough felt essential Attenborough was so adamant that Trevor play the role of Judge Broomfield that he was prepared to wait until Trevor's hectic schedule made him available for the two days it took to film his scene.

But while Sir Richard may have been ecstatic about casting Trevor in the role of the Judge, Trevor was not quite as enthusiastic, according to Patrick Newell:

> I went to Warsaw in Poland to do a TV series called *An American Sherlock Holmes* and Trevor went to India to do *Gandhi,* and he used to ring me up at four o'clock in the morning from India saying, 'Is there a part for me in your series, amigo?'
>
> I said, 'Oh come on, Trevor.'
>
> He said, 'I know your producer well. Ask him if I can be in it.'
>
> I said, 'People like you don't do television series.' But

he thought it would be a good idea! He said to me, 'I'm finished, old boy. Once you've played judges you're finished.'

I think he felt that was it for him. But he was marvellous in *Gandhi*. It's the best scene in the film. He just looks. That's all he had to do. He had this terrific presence on the screen – electrifying presence.

The same year Trevor turned up in *Sword Of The Valiant*, a remake of the 1973 *Gawain And The Green Knight* by the same director, Stephen Weeks. This new version was made to cash in on the popular sword-and-sorcery genre, and it featured a number of stars in small roles including Sean Connery as the Green Knight. The starring role went to Miles O'Keeffe, who had shot to anonymity as *Tarzan, The Ape Man* opposite Bo Derek a couple of years before.

Presumably there was something about working with Stephen Weeks that made Trevor want to repeat the experience because he turned up in Weeks' *The Bengal Lancers* which, like *Sword Of The Valiant*, doesn't appear to have surfaced in British cinemas.

In 1983 Trevor was in fine comic style once again in *The Missionary*. Written by and starring Michael Palin of *Monty Python* fame, it is set in 1906 and follows the misadventures of missionary Charles Fortescue (played by Palin) who returns to England from Africa to establish a Christian Home for Fallen Women. To raise funds he reluctantly agrees to become the lover of Lady Ames (Maggie Smith) in exchange for capital, and ends up discovering that his Fallen Women have a habit of falling into his bed.

At best the film could be described as aesthetic farce. Palin's missionary fails to hold sufficient interest and the main joke and thin story line are held up only by some great performances from the ranks of British talent such as Denholm Elliot, Michael Hordern, Maggie Smith – and Trevor Howard, seemingly having a high old time as the befuddled old husband of Lady Ames. 'In general we went for the best actors we could get,' Palin explains, 'and it made life much easier. It's like finding the right location – it relaxes you, makes you feel at ease – it's reassuring.'

Which may well sum up the attitude of too many British film-makers who use actors like Trevor as some kind of comforter, obviously believing that, if nothing else, people will enjoy the talent on display. Even American TV producers, who generally used that talent to good effect rather than just displaying it as some form of insurance policy, proved they could sometimes be of the same mind: in 1983 Trevor went to Washington to make a brief guest appearance in the ambitious mini-series *George Washington*. In 1984 Trevor, at 68, showed no signs of slowing down and he surprisingly accepted a cruise aboard the floating TV soap *Love Boat*. But his acceptance had nothing to do with the script or his role. Rather it allowed a leisurely sail through European waters while he and his co-star Colleen Dewhurst had fun at the writer's expense by putting more comedy into their roles than had been intended. And it was also a series with a huge following in America so Trevor was guaranteed an audience.

That year also he was one of many in the lavish TV production *Peter The Great* in which he portrayed Sir Isaac Newton. It was from the same stable as *Inside The Third Reich*, directed by Marvin J. Chomsky and Lawrence Schiller, and at least one star, Maximilian Schell, apparently found no shame in admitting he was unhappy with the whole project and reputedly quit before filming was complete.

Having found considerable satisfaction in doing some of the less routine offers to come his way, such as *Sir Henry At Rawlinson End*, *Light Years Away* and *Windwalker*, Trevor decided to take a further risk with *Dust*. A Belgian production, it was made in Spain (no doubt part of the attraction), and set in South Africa. Jane Birkin gave a fine performance as an unmarried woman in need of love and affection, who murders her arrogant father (played by Trevor) after he seduces the wife of his black foreman. Directed by Marion Hansel, it was the kind of film that couldn't fail to win some European award, and in 1985 the Venice Film Festival honoured it with its Silver Lion. But it was not the type of picture that could hope to compete in the commercial market, and it was never released in the UK.

It was television that allowed Trevor the luxury of both a challenging role and an audience when he played Handel in

God Rot Tunbridge Wells, written by John Osborne and directed by Tony Palmer for Channel 4. It has to be a tribute to Trevor that he was the first and only choice for Handel, and in turn Trevor desperately wanted to do it. But it was a demanding role. He had a number of very long passages of dialogue which gave him cause for some anxiety. The problem was resolved by the strategic placing of boards with his lines written on. Reading from so-called 'idiot boards' must have frustrated Trevor who was once always virtually word perfect, but in recent years he had experienced some difficulty remembering passages of dialogue. In many of his later films the problem was not manifest since most of his roles were brief. Also, shooting a film is always a stop-start process, whereas recording a play for television requires a more continuous performance. In the case of *God Rot Tunbridge Wells,* it was filmed rather than taped, but it nevertheless required stretches of continuous dialogue long enough to worry an old pro like Trevor. But then, he was almost 70, and even the most revered actors like Gielgud and Olivier have been known to forget lines in their autumn years.

Like Olivier and Gielgud, the very thought of retiring was abhorrent to Trevor. Yet, if ever there was a time when Trevor should have retired, this surely would have been it. Especially as he finished the project feeling dissatisfied with his performance. The critics agreed. Not that this indicated he couldn't act any more – every actor has to face the prospect of failure from time to time. And in Trevor's own career, while his films may not always have been exactly wonderful, anyone would be hard-pressed to pinpoint more than a couple of dud performances.

Yet he must have been aware of the passing of time and the limitation of opportunities. This he seemed to accept unwillingly as it meant never achieving the one thing he surely aimed for – overshadowing *Brief Encounter.*

Resigned to this, he continued to work, and there was plenty of it. He was one of many big names in *Shaka Zulu,* a TV mini-series filmed in South Africa in 1985. Then he co-starred with Charles Dance in *This Lightning Always Strikes Twice* for Granada Television. In the same year, 1985, Helen landed an important role in *Time After Time* with John

Gielgud and Googie Withers. It was filmed in Ireland in County Wicklow, and when director Bill Hayes suggested that Trevor play a small role, he jumped at it, eager to be with his wife in what would be their last professional appearance together.

He finished the year reunited with Ronald Neame in *Foreign Body*, a British film featuring *Passage To India* star Victor Banerjee as an itinerant Indian in London who poses as a doctor and finds his female patients demanding more than just medical attention. It was something of a throwback to the Dirk Bogarde *Doctor* films, with Trevor being his usual authoritative self as a highly respected doctor. But unhappily it was not destined for release, even in Britain: presumably the distributors felt it couldn't compete with the influx of American comedies like *Police Academy*, and the youthful antics of Michael J. Fox.

In 1986 Trevor was in an American TV film, *Christmas Eve* which heralded Hollywood star Loretta Young's return to acting after a 23-year absence from the screen. She played an eccentric millionairess determined to bring her grown-up grandchildren together for one final Christmas celebration. It was well received on American television, leaving very few dry eyes in the audience.

Trevor began his last acting year, first playing Jack Soames in *White Mischief* for Michael Radford, then as the vicar in HTV's *Hand In Glove*, and finally as the grandfather in *The Old Jest* for director Robert Knights.

By this time the old image of the man who went out for days instead of hours was replaced by one of a man who preferred a quiet drink at his local pub, The Gate. Yet even in his last years he never mellowed into what one might consider an old sage, worldly-wise and philosophical. He may not have roared very loudly any more, but he still had a youthful spirit, seemingly sensing nothing of his own mortality, yet aware of it in others. As Patrick Newell related:

I used to see him occasionally, maybe meet him in a bar. Once I met him in the local pub. The chap who ran it was ill upstairs with publican's disease. Trevor said, 'I'm just going upstairs to see him. He's in bed. He drinks too much, damn fool that he is.'

He went upstairs and gave the landlord a terrible reading about drinking. 'You shouldn't do that. It's very bad for you. You'll kill yourself if you go on drinking like that.'

But he never stopped to think about how much he drank. But then, as he said, or he reckoned, he had low blood pressure!

Well, I have no idea if Trevor had low blood pressure or not. But I did discover that he was once again enjoying a huge joke by using it as an excuse for drinking quantities of alcohol. Doctor Michael Coupland explained to me, 'There is no link between having low blood pressure and alcohol. I think Trevor Howard was kidding people when he said that.'

18

A Terrible Draught

TREVOR HAD IN fact been ordered to give up drinking by his own doctor, who must have been concerned about the condition of Trevor's liver. If newspaper reports are to be believed, he consumed a bottle of Scotch every day. But Trevor disobeyed his doctor: he always managed to excuse his drinking and once said, 'I know I drink too much but that helps me to give the kind of performance I think the public wants.' And, 'People complain that I play too many army officers. Well, the army officers I knew drank, too.'

Show business writer Minty Clinch had met and interviewed Trevor on the set of *White Mischief* and had noted that he seemed ill. She had the impression of someone who had lived life to the full but who was now at the close of it. By New Year 1988 he was jaundiced and suffering from influenza. His jaundiced condition most certainly weakened his resistance and bronchitis set it.

The rigours of a full life – a sometimes hard-living life – had taken its toll. His body had done just about as much as it could haved hoped to do over the previous 71 years. As his condition deteriorated and breathing became more difficult, he was taken to hospital and given oxygen. Helen stayed at his side and was there when, on 7 January, he died peacefully.

FAREWELL TO HOWARD THE HELLRAISER – that was the headline over the *Daily Mirror*'s obituary the day after Trevor Howard died. He'd been right when he told me that that was how he'd be remembered when his time came.

'Hellraiser Trevor Howard died more peacefully than he had lived,' the story began. It was in part true. His going was more peaceful than the getting there had ever been.

News of his death came as a total shock. Patrick Newell said:

I was in Zurich and saw his name come up on the news, and I thought 'What's he been up to?' and I looked again and they said he was dead. It was as though someone had hit me over the head. It was a really big shock.

Like everyone else, I know hundreds of people who die, and you always think 'That's terrible', but there are some people who leave a draught. Trevor's passing left a terrible draught which no one else can fill. He was one of those people who always made you feel a sort of security – to know that there are still people like that making films that, with any luck at all, you might meet again on the set and learn something else from – because you can only learn from someone like Trevor.

I was very sad about it and didn't go to the funeral because, knowing what private people he and Helen always were, I assumed it would be a very private funeral and I didn't want to intrude.

The funeral took place on 13 January at Hendon crematorium. Despite the driving rain, it was a stylish happy send-off with a taped recording of *Revival* by Chris Barber's jazz band played over the proceedings. Helen made no apologies for her choice of music: 'He was mad about traditional jazz and I know that he would have wanted to go out on a happy note.'

Like Patrick, many of Trevor's fellow actors who liked and admired him so much had stayed away, intent on keeping the private service from turning into a star-studded event, but there were flowers sent by many, including Jean Simmons and Sir John Gielgud. Outside the small chapel a respectful handful of fans gathered under umbrellas.

After the service Helen led the mourners to Trevor's local pub for a booze-up that Trevor would have undoubtedly approved of.

Shortly before he died, Trevor Howard had started a scholarship scheme at his old school, Clifton College, to help some of the school's poorer pupils. In his will he left £100,000 for the scholarship. The College's headmaster, Mr Stuart Andrews, said, 'It was a very kind and generous gesture.' It was more than that. He undoubtedly had more than loyalty for the school that had given him an education. He had roots there. He loved the place. It had been his home.

The rest of his £3 million fortune went, naturally, to Helen. Speaking publicly for the first time since Trevor's death, she said, 'I would happily give up all the money just to get Trevor back. It all means nothing without him.' She now lives, as she has for many years, a private life, still in Arkley and still acting. She and Trevor were never a traditional show-biz couple. While he made headlines, she remained in the background, and yet they were nevertheless a couple, much loved by friends and acquaintances. Whenever anyone speaks about Trevor Howard, Helen's name is inevitably brought up because anyone who knew them at all were never less than impressed by a virtually perfect match. Those who were kind enough to impart to me their own stories and impressions of Trevor have almost invariably described her in terms as endearing as those with which they describe Trevor.

Shortly after I began work on this book Patrick Newell, who was so enthusiastic in talking about Trevor, died. One thing he had said to me about Trevor's passing was, 'If there is a heaven and Trevor made it there, I can imagine he'd find the nearest bar, buy St Peter a drink and say, "Look here, amigo, do you play cricket?" '

If Patrick also made it there, and saw an angel with a drink in one hand, a cricket bat in the other and tapping his foot to the strains of an angelic jazz band, that would be Trevor Howard.

FILMOGRAPHY

*   *   *   *   *   *   *   *   *

(Date denotes year of release)

1944

The Way Ahead GFD/Two Cities. David Niven, Stanley Holloway,
Raymond Huntley, William Hartnell, James Donald, John
Laurie, Leslie Dwyer, Hugh Burden, Jimmy Hanley, Renée
Asherson, Penelope Dudley Ward, Reginald Tate, Leo Genn,
Mary Jerrold, Peter Ustinov. (Trevor Howard appeared much
further down the cast list.) Directed by Carol Reed.

1945

The Way To The Stars (US title: *Johnny In The Clouds*) Two Cities. John
Mills, Rosamund John, Michael Redgrave, Douglas
Montgomery, Basil Radford, Stanley Holloway, Joyce Carey,
Renée Asherson, Felix Aylmer, Bonar Colleano, Trevor
Howard, Jean Simmons. Directed by Anthony Asquith.

Brief Encounter Cineguild. Celia Johnson, Trevor Howard, Stanley
Holloway, Joyce Carey, Cyril Raymond. Directed by David
Lean.

I See A Dark Stranger (US title: *The Adventuress*) GFD/Individual.
Deborah Kerr, Trevor Howard, Raymond Huntley, Norman
Shelley, Michael Howard, Brenda Bruce. Directed by Frank
Launder.

1946

Green For Danger Rank/Individual. Alastair Sim, Sally Gray,
Rosamund John, Trevor Howard, Leo Genn, Megs Jenkins,
Judy Campbell. Directed by Sidney Gilliat.

1947

So Well Remembered RKO/Alliance. John Mills, Martha Scott, Trevor Howard, Patricia Roc, Richard Carlson. Directed by Edward Dmytryk.

They Made Me A Fugitive (US title: *I Became A Criminal*) Warner/ Alliance. Trevor Howard, Sally Gray, Griffin Jones, René Ray, Mary Merrall, Vida Hope, Ballard Berkley, Phyllis Robins. Directed by Alberto Cavalcanti.

1948

The Passionate Friends (US title: *One Woman's Story*) GFD/Cineguild. Ann Todd, Trevor Howard, Claude Rains, Betty Ann Davies, Isabel Dean, Arthur Howard, Wilfrid Hyde White. Directed by David Lean.

1949

The Third Man British Lion/London Films/David O. Selznick/ Alexander Korda. Joseph Cotten, Trevor Howard, Alida Valli, Orson Welles, Bernard Lee, Wilfrid Hyde White, Ernst Deutsch. Directed by Carol Reed.

The Golden Salamander GFD/Pinewood. Trevor Howard, Anouk Aimée, Herbert Lom, Miles Malleson, Walter Rilla, Jacques Sernas, Wilfrid Hyde White, Peter Copley. Directed by Ronald Neame.

1950

Odette Herbert Wilcox. Anna Neagle, Trevor Howard, Peter Ustinov, Marius Goring. Directed by Herbert Wilcox.

The Clouded Yellow Sydney and Betty Box. Trevor Howard, Jean Simmons, Barry Jones, Sonia Dresdel, Maxwell Reed, Kenneth More, André Morell. Directed by Ralph Thomas.

1951

An Outcast Of The Islands London Films. Trevor Howard, Ralph Richardson, Kerima, Robert Morley, Wendy Hiller, George Coulouris, Frederick Valk, Wilfrid Hyde White, Betty Ann Davies. Directed by Carol Reed.

1952

The Gift Horse (US title: *Glory At Sea*) British Lion/Molton. Trevor Howard, Richard Attenborough, Sonny Tufts, James Donald, Joan Rice, Bernard Lee, Dora Bryan, Hugh Williams, Robin Bailey. Directed by Compton Bennett.

1953

The Heart Of The Matter British Lion/London Films. Trevor Howard, Maria Schell, Elizabeth Allan, Denholm Elliott, Peter Finch, Gerard Dury, George Coulouris, Earl Cameron, Michael Hordern. Directed by George More O'Ferrall.

The Stranger's Hand British Lion. Trevor Howard, Richard O'Sullivan, Francis L. Sullivan, Alida Valli, Eduardo Ciannelli, Richard Basehart, Stephen Murray. Directed by Mario Soldati.

1954

The Lovers Of Lisbon EGC/Fides. Daniel Gélin, Françoise Arnoul, Trevor Howard, Ginette Leclerc, Marcel Dalio. Directed by Henri Verneuil.

1955

Cockleshell Heroes Columbia/Warwick. José Ferrer, Trevor Howard, Dora Bryan, Victor Madden, Anthony Newley, Peter Arne, David Lodge, Water Fitzgerald, Beatrice Campbell. Directed by José Ferrer.

1956

Run For The Sun United Artists/Russ-field. Richard Widmark, Jane Greer, Trevor Howard, Peter Van Eyck, Carlos Henning. Directed by Roy Boulting.

Around The World In Eighty Days United Artists/Michael Todd. David Niven, Cantinflas, Robert Newton, Shirley MacLaine and a huge international cast among which was Trevor Howard. Directed by Michael Anderson.

1957

Manuela (US title: *Stowaway Girl*) British Lion. Trevor Howard, Elsa Martinelli, Pedro Armedariz, Donald Pleasence. Directed by Guy Hamilton.

Interpol (US title: *Pickup Alley*) Columbia/Warwick. Victor Mature, Anita Ekberg, Trevor Howard, Bonar Colleano. Directed by John Gilling.

1958

The Key (Columbia/Open Road. William Holden, Sophia Loren, Trevor Howard, Oscar Homolka, Kieron Moore. Directed by Carol Reed.

The Roots Of Heaven 20th-Century Fox. Trevor Howard, Juliette Greco, Errol Flynn, Eddie Albert, Orson Welles, Paul Lukas, Herbert Lom. Directed by John Huston.

1960

Sons And Lovers 20th-Century Fox. Dean Stockwell, Trevor Howard, Wendy Hiller, Mary Ure, Heather Sears, William Lucas, Donald Pleasence, Ernest Thesiger. Directed by Jack Cardiff.

1962

Moment Of Danger (US title: *Malaga*) ABPC/Douglas Fairbanks Jnr. Trevor Howard, Dorothy Dandridge, Edmund Purdom, Michael Hordern, Paul Stassino. Directed by Laslo Benedek.

Mutiny On The Bounty MGM/Arcola. Trevor Howard, Marlon Brando, Richard Harris, Hugh Griffith, Tarita, Richard Haydn, Percy Herbert, Duncan Lamont, Gordon Jackson, Chips Rafferty, Noel Purcell. Directed by Lewis Milestone.

The Lion 20th-Century Fox. William Holden, Trevor Howard, Capucine, Pamela Franklin, Samuel Romboh, Christopher Agunda. Directed by Jack Cardiff.

1964

Man In The Middle 20th-Century Fox. Robert Mitchum, Trevor Howard, Keenan Wynn, Barry Sullivan, France Nuyen, Alexander Knox. Directed by Guy Hamilton.

Father Goose Universal-International/Granox. Cary Grant, Leslie Caron, Trevor Howard, Jack Good, Nicole Felsette. Directed by Ralph Nelson.

1965

Operation Crossbow MGM/Carlo Ponti. George Peppard, Tom Courtenay, John Mills, Sophia Loren, Lilli Palmer, Anthony Quayle, Patrick Wymark, Jeremy Kemp, Paul Henreid, Trevor Howard, Sylvia Sims, Richard Todd. Directed by Michael Anderson.

Von Ryan's Express 20th-Century Fox. Frank Sinatra, Trevor Howard, Sergio Fantoni, Edward Mulhare, Brad Dexter, John Leyton, Wolfgang Preiss, James Brolin. Directed by Mark Robson.

The Saboteur, Code Name Morituri 20th-Century Fox/Arcola/Colony. Yul Brynner, Marlon Brando, Trevor Howard, Janet Margolin, Wally Cox, William Redfield, Carl Esmond. Directed by Bernhard Wicki.

The Liquidator MGM. Rod Taylor, Trevor Howard, David Tomlinson, Jill St John, Wilfrid Hyde White, Derek Nimmo, Eric Sykes, Akim Tamiroff. Directed by Jack Cardiff.

Danger Grows Wild (See under **Television Productions(** *The Poppy Is Also A Flower*)

1967

Triple Cross Warner/Cineurop. Christopher Plummer, Yul Brynner, Trevor Howard, Romy Schneider, Gert Frobe, Claudine Auger. Directed by Terence Young.

The Long Duel Rank. Trevor Howard, Yul Brynner, Harry Andrews, Charlotte Rampling, Virginia North, Andrew Keir, Laurence Naismith, Maurice Denham, Patrick Newell. Directed by Ken Annakin.

Pretty Polly (US title: *A Matter Of Innocence*) Universal. Hayley Mills, Trevor Howard, Shashi Kapoor, Brenda de Banzie, Dick Patterson. Directed by Guy Green.

The Charge Of The Light Brigade United Artists/Woodfall. Trevor Howard, John Gielgud, David Hemmings, Vanessa Redgrave, Jill Bennett, Harry Andrews, Peter Bowles, Mark Burns. Directed by Tony Richardson.

1969

The Battle Of Britain United Artists. Laurence Olivier, Robert Shaw, Michael Caine, Christopher Plummer, Kenneth More, Susannah York, Trevor Howard, Ralph Richardson, Patrick Wymark, Curt Jurgens, Michael Redgrave, Nigel Patrick, Robert Flemyng, Edward Fox, Ian McShane. Directed by Guy Hamilton.

Twinky Rank. Charles Bronson, Susan George, Trevor Howard, Michael Craig, Honor Blackman, Robert Morley, Jack Hawkins. Directed by Richard Donner.

1970

Ryan's Daughter MGM. Sarah Miles, Robert Mitchum, Christopher Jones, John Mills, Trevor Howard, Leo McKern, Barry Foster. Directed by David Lean.

1971

Catch Me A Spy Ludgate/Capitole/Bryna. Kirk Douglas, Trevor Howard, Tom Courtenay, Marlene Jobert, Patrick Mower. Directed by Dick Clement.

The Night Visitor. Max Von Sydow, Liv Ullmann, Trevor Howard, Per Oscarsson, Rupert Davies. Directed by Laslo Benedek.

Mary Queen Of Scots Universal. Vanessa Redgrave, Glenda Jackson, Trevor Howard, Patrick McGoohan, Nigel Davenport, Timothy Dalton, Daniel Massey, Ian Holm. Directed by Charles Jarrott.

1972

The Offense United Artists. Sean Connery, Trevor Howard, Ian Bannen, Vivien Merchant, Derek Newark. Directed by Sidney Lumet.

Ludwig Studio. Helmut Berger, Romy Schneider, Trevor Howard, Silvana Magnano, Helmut Griem, Nora Ricci, Gert Frobe, John Moulder Brown. Directed by Luchino Visconti.

Pope Joan (reissued in US as *The Devil's Imposter*) Big City Productions/Kurt Unger. Liv Ullmann, Trevor Howard, Olivia de Havilland, Maximilian Schell, Keir Dullea, Robert Beatty, Franco Nero, Patrick Magee. Directed by Michael Anderson.

1973

A Doll's House World Film Services/Les Films de la Boetie. Jane
Fonda, David Warner, Trevor Howard, Edward Fox, Delphine
Seyrig, Anna Wing. Directed by Joseph Losey.

Craze EMI. Jack Palance, Diana Dors, Julie Ege, Edith Evans,
Hugh Griffith, Trevor Howard, Michael Jayston, Suzy
Kendall, Martin Potter, Percy Herbert, Kathleen Byron.
Directed by Freddie Francis.

1974

Eleven Harrowhouse 20th-Century Fox. Charles Grodin, James
Mason, Trevor Howard, John Gielgud, Candice Bergen, Peter
Vaughan, Helen Cherry, Jack Watson, Jack Watling. Directed
by Aram Avakian.

Persecution Tyburn. Lana Turner, Ralph Bates, Olga Georges-Picot,
Trevor Howard, Suzan Farmer, Ronald Howard, Patrick
Allen. Directed by Don Chaffey.

1975

Conduct Unbecoming British Lion. Michael York, Stacy Keach, Trevor
Howard, Christopher Plummer, Richard Attenborough,
Susannah York, James Faulkner, James Donald. Directed by
Michael Anderson.

Hennessy AIP/Marseilles. Rod Steiger, Richard Johnson, Lee
Remick, Trevor Howard, Eric Porter, Peter Egan. Directed by
Don Sharp.

Death In The Sun Trevor Howard, Christopher Lee. Directed by
Jurgen Goslar. (Not released.)

1976

The Bawdy Adventures of Tom Jones Universal. Nicky Henson, Trevor
Howard, Terry-Thomas, Arthur Lowe, Georgia Brown, Joan
Collins. Directed by Cliff Owen.

Aces High EMI. Malcolm McDowell, Christopher Plummer, Simon Ward, Peter Firth, John Gielgud, Trevor Howard, Richard Johnson, Ray Milland. Directed by Jack Gold.

Eliza Fraser. Susannah York, Trevor Howard. Directed by Tim Burstall.

1977

The Last Remake Of Beau Geste Universal. Marty Feldman, Michael York, Ann-Margret, Peter Ustinov, Trevor Howard, James Earl Jones, Henry Gibson, Terry-Thomas, Roy Kinnear, Spike Milligan, Hugh Griffith, Irene Handl. Directed by Marty Feldman.

1978

Slavers. Trevor Howard, Ron Ely, Britt Ekland, Jurgen Goslar, Ray Milland. Directed by Jurgen Goslar.

Superman – The Movie Warner Bros/Alexander Salkind. Marlon Brando, Christopher Reeve, Margot Kidder, Jackie Cooper, Gene Hackman, Glenn Ford, Phyllis Thaxter, Trevor Howard, Ned Beatty, Susannah York, Valerie Perrine, Harry Andrews. Directed by Richard Donner.

Stevie First Artists/Grand Metropolitan. Glenda Jackson, Mona Washbourne, Trevor Howard, Alec McGowen. Directed by Robert Enders.

1979

Hurricane Jason Robards, Mia Farrow, Dayton Ka'ne, Max von Sydow, Trevor Howard. Directed by Jan Troell.

Meteor Movielab. Sean Connery, Natalie Wood, Karl Malden, Brian Keith, Martin Landau, Trevor Howard, Henry Fonda. Directed by Ronald Neame.

1980

The Sea Wolves Euan Lloyd. Gregory Peck, Roger Moore, Trevor Howard, David Niven, Barbara Kellerman, Patrick MacNee, Patrick Allen. Directed by Andrew V. McLaglen.

Windwalker Pacific International Enterprises. Trevor Howard, Nick

Ramus, James Remar, Serene Hedin, Dusty Iron Wing McCrea. Directed by Kieth Merrill.

Sir Henry At Rawlinson End Charisma. Trevor Howard, Patrick Magee, Denise Coffey, J.G. Devlin. Directed by Steve Roberts.

1981

Light Years Away Trevor Howard, Mick Ford, Bernice Stegers, Henri Vorogeux. Directed by Alain Tanner.

1982

Gandhi Columbia/Goldcrest. Ben Kingsley, Candice Bergen, Edward Fox, John Mills, John Gielgud, Trevor Howard, Martin Sheen, Ian Charleson. Directed by Richard Attenborough.

Sword Of The Valiant Miles O'Keefe, Cyrielle Claire, Leigh Lawson, Sean Connery, Trevor Howard, Peter Cushing. Directed by Stephen Weeks.

The Missionary Handmade. Michael Palin, Maggie Smith, Denholm Elliott, Phoebe Nicholls, Rosamund Greenwood, Michael Hordern, Trevor Howard. Directed by Richard Locraine.

1984

Dust Jane Birkin, Trevor Howard; John Matshikiza, Nadine Unwampa, Lourdes Christina Sayo, Rene Diaz. Directed by Marion Hansel.

1986

Foreign Body Victor Banerjee, Warren Mitchell, Trevor Howard, Geraldine McEwan, Amanda Donohoe, Denis Quilley, Eve Ferret, Anna Massey. Directed by Ronald Neame.

1987

The Old Jest Directed by Robert Knights.

1988

White Mischief Directed by Michael Radford.

STAGE PLAYS

*   *   *   *   *   *   *   *   *

1934

Revolt In A Reformatory Gate Theatre.
The Drums Begin Embassy Theatre.
Androcles And The Lion Winter Garden Theatre.
The Faithful Westminster Theatre.
Alien Corn Westminster Theatre.

1935

The Rivals Q Theatre.
Crime And Punishment Embassy Theatre.
Aren't We All? Royal Court Theatre.
Justice Playhouse.
Skin Game Playhouse.
A Family Man Playhouse.
Lady Patricia Westminster Theatre.
Legend Of Yesterday Aldwych.
Timon Of Athens Westminster Theatre.

1936

French Without Tears Criterion Theatre.

1937

Waters Of Jordan Sunday Night Repertory at Arts Theatre.

1938

A Star Comes Home Arts Theatre.

1939

Private Lives With the Colchester Repertory Company.
Cinderella With The Colchester Repertory Company.

1940

The Importance Of Being Earnest With the Harrogate White Rose
Players.
Rope Also directed while stationed at Officer Cadet Training Unit in
Dunbar, Scotland.

1943

The Recruiting Officer Arts Theatre.

1944

A Soldier For Christmas Wyndhams Theatre.
Anna Christie Arts Theatre.

1947

The Taming Of The Shrew On tour including Edinburgh, Oxford and
London at the New Theatre.

1953

The Devil's General Savoy.

1954

The Cherry Orchard Lyric Theatre.

1962

Two Stars For Comfort Garrick Theatre.

1964

The Father Theatre Royal, Brighton; Piccadilly Theatre; Queens Theatre.

1972

Separate Tables (excerpt) Charity performance.

1974

Waltz Of The Toreadors Haymarket Theatre.

1976

The Scenario Royal Alexandra Theatre, Toronto, Canada.

TELEVISION PRODUCTIONS

*   *   *   *   *   *   *   *   *

1954

Still Life (Tonight At 8.30 series) Also with Ginger Rogers. Directed by Otto Preminger.

The Flower Of Pride Also with Geraldine Fitzgerald. Directed by Franklin Schaffner.

1962

Hedda Gabler Also with Ingrid Bergman, Ralph Richardson, Michael Redgrave. Directed by Alex Segal.

1963

The Invincible Mr Disraeli Also with Greer Garson, Kate Reid, Hurd Hatfield, Denholm Elliott, Geoffrey Keen. Directed by George Schaefer.

1965

The Poppy Is Also A Flower. (Released theatrically as *Danger Grows Wild*) Also with E.G. Marshall, Stephen Boyd, Eli Wallach, Marcello Mastroianni, Angie Dickinson, Rita Hayworth, Yul Brynner, Trini Lopez, Gilbert Roland, Bessie Love, Jack Hawkins. Directed by Terence Young.

Eagle In A Cage Also with Pamela Franklin. Directed by George Schaefer.

1973

Catholics Also with Martin Sheen, Raf Vallone, Cyril Cusack, Andrew Keir, Michael Gambon, Leon Vitale. Directed by Jack Gold.

1975

The Count Of Monte Cristo. (Released theatrically in UK) Also with Richard Chamberlain, Tony Curtis, Louis Jourdan, Donald Pleasence, Taryn Power. Directed by David Greene.

1978

Easterman (Scorpion Tales series) Also with Don Henderson. Directed by David Reid.

1979

Night Flight Also with Bo Svenson, Celine Lomez. Directed by Desmond Davis.

The Shillingbury Blowers Also with Robin Nedwell, Diane Keen, Jack Douglas, Sam Kydd, John LeMesurier, Patrick Newell. Directed by Val Guest.

1980

Staying On Also with Celia Johnson. Directed by Silvio Narizzano.

1981

No Country For Old Men Also with Cyril Cusack. Directed by Tristam Powell.

1983

Inside The Third Reich Also with Rutger Hauer, John Gielgud, Maria Schell, Derek Jacobi, Randy Quaid, Stephen Collins, Ian Holm, Elke Sommer, Robert Vaughn. Directed by Marvin J. Chomsky.

The Deadly Game Also with George Segal, Robert Morley, Emlyn Williams, Alan Webb. Directed by George Schaefer.

George Washington (Shown in UK in 1988) Directed by Buz Pulick.

1984

The Love Boat Also with Colleen Dewhurst.

God Rot Tunbridge Wells Directed by Tony Palmer.

1985

Time After Time Also with John Gielgud, Helen Cherry, Googie Withers, Brenda Bruce. Directed by Bill Hayes.

This Lightning Always Strikes Twice Also with Charles Dance. Directed by David Carson.

1986

Peter The Great Directed by Marvin J. Chomsky and Lawrence Schiller.

Shaka Zulu Also with Christopher Lee, Edward Fox. Directed by Bill Faure.

Christmas Eve Also with Loretta Young, Ron Liebman, Arthur Hill, Patrick Cassidy, Season Hubley, Kate Reid. Directed by Stuart Cooper.

1987

Hand In Glove For HTV.

BIBLIOGRAPHY

*   *   *   *   *   *   *   *   *

(All titles refer to books unless otherwise stated.)

Bergman, Ingrid and Burgess Alan, *Ingrid Bergman: My Story*. Dell 1981.

Eells, George, *Robert Mitchum*. Franklin Watts 1984.

Faulkner, Trader, *Peter Finch*. Taplinger 1980.

Guiles, Fred Lawrence, *Jane Fonda*. Pinnacle 1983.

Hall, William, *Trevor Howard – A Photoplay Tribute* (article), *Photoplay*, Argus Specialist Publications, April 1988.

Halliwell, Leslie, *Halliwell's Film Guide* (4th Edition). Scribner 1985.

Hawkins, Jack, *Anything For A Quiet Life*. Stein and Day 1974.

Higham, Charles, *Errol Flynn: The Untold Story*. Doubleday 1980.

Hudgins, Morgan, *Mutiny On The Bounty* (souvenir brochure). MGM 1962.

Knight, Vivienne, *Trevor Howard: A Gentleman and A Player*, Muller, Blond & White 1986; Sphere 1988.

Mayo, Robert, *The Charge Of The Light Brigade* (souvenir brochure). James Kantor and Associates 1968.

Mills, John, *Up In The Clouds*. Ticknor & Fields 1981

More, Kenneth, *More Or Less*. Hodder and Stoughton 1978.

Morley, Sheridan, *Theatre 74*. Hutchinson 1974.

Morley, Sheridan, *The Other Side Of The Moon*. Harper & Row 1985.

Mosely, Roy, *Rex Harrison*. New English Library 1987.

Nolan, William F., *John Huston – King Rebel*. Sherbourne Press 1965.

Pettigrew, Terence, *Trevor Howard* (article). *Photoplay*, Argus Press, August 1979.

Shipman, David, *The Great Movie Stars – The International Years*. Hill & Wang 1981.

Thomas, Bob, *Brando*. W.H. Allen 1973.

Vermilye, Jerry, *Cary Grant*. Galahad Books 1973.

Willis, John, *The Battle of Britain* (souvenir brochure). Sackville Publishing 1969.

Index